# EXPRESSIVE PROCESSES IN GROUP COUNSELING

# EXPRESSIVE PROCESSES IN GROUP COUNSELING

## Theory and Practice

NINA W. BROWN

PRAEGER

Westport, Connecticut
London

**Library of Congress Cataloging-in-Publication Data**

Brown, Nina W.
Expressive processes in group counseling : theory and practice / Nina W. Brown
p. cm.
Includes bibliographical references and index.
ISBN 0–275–95509–5 (alk. paper)
1. Group counseling. 2. Group psychotherapy. 3. Cross-cultural counseling. I. Title.
BF637.C6B763 1996
158′.35—dc20 95–45417



British Library Cataloguing in Publication Data is available.



Library of Congress Catalog Card Number: 95–45417
ISBN: 0–275–95509–5

First published in 1996

Praeger Publishers, 88 Post Road West, Westport, CT 06881
An imprint of Greenwood Publishing Group, Inc.

Printed in the United States of America

The paper used in this book complies with the Permanent Paper Standard issued by the National Information Standards Organization (Z39.48–1984).

10 9 8 7 6 5 4 3 2 1

# CONTENTS

# 1

# FOUNDATIONS

## PURPOSE OF BOOK

### Overview

*Theory and Practice for Expressive Processes in Group Therapy* presents the theory and practice of using indirect ways, such as art, to help group members access and use emotionally laden personal material in counseling and therapy. Expressive techniques are relatively easy to use in superficial ways. However, if their benefits are to be maximized, the group leader needs to have a firm theoretical base for using them, an understanding of procedures and processes they entail, selecting of appropriate processes, applications to specific conditions, and knowledge of a variety of processes from which to choose. While this book is not all-inclusive, it does seek to provide adequate coverage.

Chapters 1 through 6 give a background for use of expressive processes in group therapy and counseling. These chapters cover preparation of the leader, cross-cultural considerations, therapeutic attitude, observational skills, role of theory, selection and use techniques, and applications to problem behaviors. Chapters 7 through 12 address art, imagery, dreams, guided writing, fairy tales and movement expressive processes. Each chapter has an overview of theory and rationale for the group of techniques, a process for using them in groups, and specific examples.

### Chapter 1

"Foundations" begins with an overview, defines and explains uses of expressive processes, and discusses the basic preparation group leaders need and cross-cultural considerations. Uses include benefits for both the individual and the group process. Group leaders are cautioned against using techniques indiscriminately, or just for the sake of using them, and are encouraged to become adequately prepared in the backgrounds, procedures, and processes for each group of techniques.

Cross-cultural considerations are discussed extensively with a focus on encouraging the group leader to develop cultural sensitivity, and to consider the development of cultural sensitivity as an ongoing process. The discussion begins with listing the major cross-cultural errors that can cause misunderstandings, be confusing, and be offensive. Because cultural influences are often subtle, they are not always recognized as part of communication problems. Also given are steps the leader can use to develop cultural sensitivity, and four phases of cultural growth.

### Chapter 2

"Maximizing Outcomes" provides suggestions for group leaders and members that lead to getting the most out of the experiences. The discussion on counselors' factors gives a rationale for paying attention to their own physical condition and psychological attitude, taking pains to develop a therapeutic relationship prior to initiating expressive processes, assets the counselor brings to using these techniques; the need for a here and now focus; and ethical considerations. Group members are to be encouraged to do the following to maximize benefits: have a willingness to participate, engage in self-disclosure, openly express their feelings and emotions, and seek to be honest with self and others. Much of the discussion emphasizes the inner state of being, such as willingness to take psychological risks and motivation, and highlights the level and intensity of these experiences. Group leaders are also given guidelines for providing feedback.

### Chapter 3

"Nonverbal Communication" has an extensive discussion on observing and understanding nonverbal behaviors. Categories of behaviors that provide cues are listed: bodily behaviors such as posture and facial expressions; voice related behaviors, such as tone and inflection; observable autonomic physiological responses, such as sweating and physical characteristics; and general appearance. Purposes of nonverbal messages and functions are also discussed. Although examples of gestures are provided, it is emphasized that these should be observed in clusters and not as isolated events.

### Chapter 4

"Theories" gives an overview of major theories considered by the author to have implications that underline using expressive processes. The theories presented are not all-inclusive, and the reader is encouraged to use other theories as they appear appropriate. The theories discussed are object relations, gestalt, existential, person-centered, and Jungian. Each theory provides a perspective and framework to describe and understand human growth and development, and give suggestions for problem or issue identifications and strategies for resolution or solution.

### Chapter 5

"Guidelines" focuses on factors to be considered when selecting expressive processes. Ethical considerations, such as the need for confidentiality, informed consent, the psychological condition of group members, and involuntary membership, are emphasized. Other topics include planning, preparation, description of procedures and tasks and, most important, processing of the experience. The emphasis for this chapter is to help the leader understand constraints in order to protect group members as they participate in these activities.

### Chapter 6

"Applications" discusses varied ways of using expressive processes for different problems/issues/concerns. It begins with a discussion of the advantage of using expressive processes with difficult member behaviors, such as monopolizing, hostility and anger, silence, and story telling. Group problem behaviors that can benefit from using expressive processes are presented; for example, collusion, inability to focus on feelings, and resistance. A model for conceptualizing feelings and experiences as layers is discussed along with group issues that expressive processes can facilitate in reaching resolution, such as conflict, intimacy, dependency, and fears. Other applications, such as pregroup preparation of members, as the group begins, self-awareness, the "shadow" side of self; and termination, are presented.

### Chapter 7

"Art" presents guidelines for using art expressive processes: the process for planning, material selection, appropriateness for members, procedures, and processing of the experience. Also presented are examples of using art expressive processes during different stages of group development. Thirteen art expressive processes are described.

### Chapter 8

"Imagery" discusses the background, definitions, advantages, types, guidelines, and procedures for using guided imagery in group counseling. Also presented are techniques for structuring imagery experiences, considerations for using them, understanding of what emerged, and recognition of when a member is stuck. Examples of twenty-five imagery exercises from the literature are presented.

### Chapter 9

"Dreams" begins with a review of various theoretical approaches to understanding and analyzing dreams. Among dream interpretations presented are phenomenological, transpersonal, person-centered, and gestalt. A brief discussion of Freud's and Jung's methods for understanding dreams is presented. Seven methods for analyzing dreams derived from literature reviews are described; the dream appreciation group, dream understanding exercise, dream mapping, dream analysis in a group, the prolucid semantics technique, dream enlargements, and symbols as metaphors. Four additional methods described are, cinquain, draw a dream, dream symbol expansion, and constructive use for nightmares.

### Chapter 10

"Writing" presents strategies for using both reading and writing. Guidelines for bibliotherapy are given with particular emphasis on its use in group counseling. Advantages and disadvantages of using writing expressive processes are presented, along with suggestions for eleven exercises, such as journals and diaries; an intensive journal; autobiography; and dialogues.

### Chapter 11

"Fairy Tales" begins with a theoretical foundation for using fairy tales as expressive processes. An example of using fairy tales with adolescents and adults is presented. Further discussions are on messages in fairy tales, general process used in developing a fairy tale, use of fairy tales in counseling, themes and symbols of selected fairy tales, and processing of the experience.

### Chapter 12

"Movement" considers how use of the body can express inner and outer experiencing. When movement is used as an expressive process the assumption is that the movements initiated, the form or shape the body takes, and the nonverbal responses to external stimuli reflect the inner emotional state. The ways one moves, stands, and/or gestures are more accurate messages of feelings and emotions than are the words spoken.

Schutz (1967) notes that the language is rich in the variety of ways that feelings and behavior are expressed in terms of the body and bodily functions. Terms such as "pain in the neck," "don't get in my hair," " spine tingling," "stiff upper lip," "lose your head," "can't stomach it," and "turn the other cheek" are a few examples. Thus, the body is seen as a rich source of information about an individual.

The chapter presents theoretical perspectives for movement and dance, purposes, guidelines for initiating exercises, and ten examples of movement exercises.

## DEFINITIONS OF EXPRESSIVE PROCESSES

Robbins (1980) proposes that "the essence of expressive therapy lies in process rather than in technique, for the therapy occurs though the vehicle of psychic play rather than in the actual products of artistic production." Process is emphasized over technique and product. It is also assumed that expressive processes let the individual more easily access material that is contained on the unconscious level, or that material of which they are not fully aware. The expressive processes described in this book are art, imagery, dreams, guided writing, fairy tales, and movement.

### Art in Counseling

Art, in this book, is not intended to be used as it would if done with an art therapist. These trained professionals generally operate within a psychoanalytic framework which stresses the "need to interpret the artistic production alongside the patient's associations to it, if unconscious themes and phenomena such as transference are to be fully understood" (Walrond-Skinner, 1986). The definition used in this book is drawn from McNiff (1992), who suggests that creation and reflection of artistic products have healing properties. The artistic images that are created encourage reflection: rather than labeling or interpreting artistic products, one is encouraged "to meditate on them, tell stories about how we created them, speak to them, listen to what they have to say, dramatize them through our bodily movement, and dream about them."

### Imagery in Counseling

Freud viewed fantasy and dreams as primary process events generated by the *id*--that is, those primitive wishes and fears that are suppressed by thought and reason, which are conceptualized as functions of the ego. Jung perceived fantasy and dreams as methods that the person could use to integrate layers of "self" and to further growth. Gestalt therapists use fantasy as a means to get in touch with disowned parts of self, and with fears and anxieties that have been suppressed but still have an impact. The psychosynthesis approach views fantasy as methods of awakening potential, promoting awareness, resolving conflicts, and initiating healing. Guided imagery is described in this book as a means to increase awarenesses and tap into unrealized potentials.

### Dreams in Counseling

Freud felt that dreams represented a wish that is repressed and emerges from the unconscious disguised as symbols. Jung suggested that dreams have creative functions and that the main purpose of the dream is to communicate rather than disguise. He also postulated that dreams drew from the collective unconscious as well as the personal unconscious of the individual. Gestalt therapists consider dreams to represent fragmented parts of the self that are disowned when awake.

These and other perspectives form the basis for the presentation on using dreams as expressive processes. Dreams are considered to be bearers of personal associations and messages that appear to the dreamer in symbolic form, and are subject to that individual's personal analyses and interpretation.

### Writing in Counseling

Writing, as an expressive process, can be very fruitful for individuals in their efforts to understand themselves better. Guided writing focuses on strategies that emphasize particular areas that may contain important material or information for the individual. Writing also allows the individual to return to the product at a later time and reexperience, analyze, and/or interpret it further. Recording thoughts, feelings, emotions, and so on, as they occur helps provide a more accurate record of what transpired and was experienced than does memory. The exercises described are examples of how guided writing can be used to further the process of counseling.

Also included in the chapter are suggestions for using reading as a counseling strategy.

### Fairy Tales in Counseling

Fairy tales are not just for children. These are folk tales that hold potential for guiding growth and development at various stages throughout life. Although the circumstances may differ at different stages, the basic tasks may be the same. We encounter numerous thresholds as we develop, and fairy tales give hope and show how these thresholds can be worked through constructively. These are generic fairy tales that use symbols that can be similar across people and across age groups. The symbols in these generic fairy tales provide clues to current functioning, conflicts with self and others, possibilities for growth and problem resolution, and seed potentials.

### Movement in Counseling

"Dance-movement therapy in its expressive aspects allows for such a structure, in that the therapist enlists the cognitive functions of the ego by inviting the client to observe and feel him (her) self in the movement" (Siegel, 1980). Siegel also quotes Trudie Schoop: "When a dance therapist brings about a change in body behavior, there should be a corresponding change in the mind." American Dance Therapy defines *dance therapy* as the therapeutic use of movement to further the emotional and physical integration of the individual (*Dictionary of Psychotherapy*). Although these definitions emphasize dance, the same points can be made about use of movement as an expressive process. This book presents various ways of using movement and/or dance to help individuals become more aware of their bodies and what their movements and positioning of body and parts reveal about their self-perceptions.

## RATIONALE FOR USING EXPRESSIVE PROCESSES

### Benefits to Clients

Expressive processes can facilitate development of awarenesses for self and others, further emotional and psychological growth, promote group cohesion, and allow for spontaneity and creativity of expression. These processes, when used appropriately, facilitate both individual and group progress. The uses described in this book assume that the group leader has been prepared to lead groups but not necessarily a group that has expressive processes as its main agenda. Group leaders are not expected to be experts, such as certified art therapists; nor are the processes described to be used as they would be by a trained professional in that area. These are techniques, grounded in theory, that almost any good group leader could use to promote progress of the group. The understandings, insights, and awarenesses that emerge when they are used as described are not intended to be as in-depth as they would if a trained professional were analyzing them. However, it is assumed that in-depth analyses are not always needed for growth and development.

Expressive processes, when used as described, can help bypass defenses, allow members to access inner processes that are mainly unconscious, release creative energies, resolve dilemmas and/or impasses, relieve tension, promote healing, identify early traumas or deficits, promote awareness of suppressed or repressed feelings, express complicated and/or intense feelings, identify unresolved issues or unfinished business, and focus on essentials of an issue or event rather than getting caught up in details. They provide a mechanism whereby significant material is brought into awareness allowing group members to productively address their issues. Each of these uses will be briefly described.

### Bypass Defenses

Individuals defend the self against anxiety and/or destruction by using a variety of defense mechanisms. Many of the defenses are unconscious, appear in layers, and may resist conscious efforts to dissolve them. The fear that they defend against is too strong or ingrained to be easily overcome. The group leader also has to move carefully when confronted with defense mechanisms, and may have difficulty in identifying defenses as they may manifest themselves in layers. Defenses are very complicated and even when individuals face little or no threat they may be so accustomed to keeping defenses in place that they use them when they do not need to do so. Even when the defense is identified a group leader may find it more beneficial to give the member space and time to recognize the defense rather than the leader terming or labelling it as a defense.

Expressive processes allow defenses to be bypassed to some extent, and in a safe way. The individual determines the extent and amount of participation and is not manipulated or pushed into lowering defenses. Further, the individual decides what will be shared with the group and if the material is too sensitive, can reinstate the protective defense. However, the individual is then more aware of the use of the defense and what material it may be hiding.

When defenses are bypassed, sometimes the individual is able to access inner processes that are unconscious. Inner processes such as associations and thoughts become illuminated and their relationship or impact on current functioning becomes more apparent. While the purpose of the expressive process may not be to make the unconscious conscious, sometimes the net effect is that one becomes more aware of his or her inner world.

### Releasing Creative Energies

A lot of energy goes into suppression, repression, and denial. Expressive processes can release creative energies and free the person to be more alive, spontaneous, and creative in everyday life. Expressive processes described in this book do not require the group member to have recognized talent, and it is assumed that everyone has some creative ability whether or not it is manifested in recognizable forms, such as art or writing. Creative energies allow the person to experience life more fully, and releasing some creative energy is one of the benefits of expressive processes.

### Resolving Impasses

We are all familiar with situations and/or relationships that present us with dilemmas or impasses. Discussions, thoughts, feelings become stuck, or move in a circular pattern, going nowhere. Expressive processes can help in these instances by providing another perspective, identifying components that contribute to the "stuckness," and suggesting strategies for resolution. Group members, in particular, can become more aware of their personal contribution to the impasse or dilemma, and take steps to remedy the situation. Many times the group is stuck and members perceive it to be the behavior or attitude of one person that is making the entire group unable to proceed. The more they attack the problem, the more circular interactions and discussions become, leading to greater frustration. An expressive process used at this point can help each member to accept his or her part of the problem and, by doing so, make strides toward constructive problem-solving.

### Relieving Tension

Some measure of tension is very needed if the group is to be productive. Very relaxed groups who are too comfortable are not usually working productively. However, there are times when the tension is so intense that there is no productive work being done and/or members are in danger of being overwhelmed by the ensuing anxiety. In this instance it would be beneficial to use an expressive process to relieve some of the tension. An exercise that allows members to have fun and play would be appropriate, and would probably result in a willingness to dive back in and work harder. Another benefit for some members is that they learn to have fun and to play. They may have been mired in their problems for so long that they have forgotten how it feels to have fun and not to be overly tense.

### Building Awarenesses

One of the twelve steps of Alcoholics Anonymous is letting go. Letting go of old hurts, resentments, relationships, and so on, is a part of the healing process. However, it is very difficult to know how or when to let go. Expressive processes can facilitate awareness of those parts of life that are unproductive or destructive, and suggest how to cut oneself free. Continuing to work on a relationship that holds no promise of getting better or adding quality to one's life is not a constructive use of time, and the individual may be better served by letting go of it. Most of us hold on to things, people, attitudes, relationships, and so forth, that no longer are of value or that do not contribute to our well-being in any way. Knowing when to let go facilitates growth, development, and healing. Expressive processes in the group may allow members to let the awareness emerge for both productive and unproductive parts of their lives.

### Recalling Earlier Events

Repression and denial contribute to forgetting early traumas or deficiencies that continue to impact functioning. Expressive processes can facilitate the gradual unfolding of remembering these so that they can become material for examination and growth. The key phrase is "gradual unfolding." This is important because early traumas or deficits can be so emotionally overwhelming as to engulf the individual. When used as described in this book, expressive processes guard against this by empowering the individual to determine what to explore and to control what emerges. While more may emerge than anticipated, it is unusual for so much material to emerge that the individual feels engulfed. Adequate processing of expressive processes also provides a safety measure to protect individuals. When these early experiences are allowed to unfold, the individual is more apt to continue to explore them; this, in turn, leads to a greater ability to work through them.

### Expressing Feelings and Emotions

Group members often suppress persistent feelings in the group and this leads to an impasse. In addition, members may suppress or repress significant feelings about personal issues. Expressive processes can promote awareness of suppressed or repressed feelings, and promote a heightened awareness of the impact on current functioning and/or relationships. Increasing awareness of significant feelings allows members to begin to express them, control them, and work through them to promote growth and development.

Many group members do not know appropriate ways to express complicated feelings and emotions. For example, grief and mourning can involve feelings of sadness, abandonment, anger, and relief. Guilt and shame may result from conflicting feelings about the lost person or relationship. Expressive processes help individuals appropriately express the many, and sometimes conflicting, feelings and emotions. When they are used in a group setting, the group therapeutic factor of universality can also emerge. However, catharsis, in and of itself, is considered to be a therapeutic factor in group and expressive processes can facilitate its emergence.

### Unfinished Business

Identification of unresolved issues and/or unfinished business can also be facilitated by using expressive processes. Many individuals are unaware of the continuing impact of unresolved issues and unfinished business. Some feel, on a conscious level, that a particular issue may have been resolved or a piece of business finished. An expressive process makes them aware not only that it has not been resolved or finished, but that it continues to have a negative influence on their functioning and relationships. This awareness is another step on the way to resolving and finishing.

### Focus on Essentials

One of the most important uses of expressive processes in group counseling is to focus on essentials of an issue. Quite often members become caught up in details and neglect essentials. This may be true for more than one member in the group, and, in order to block story telling, an appropriate expressive process that highlights the linked essentials for members would be beneficial. Expressive processes can be used effectively to block intellectualizing, avoidance, story telling, and inability to accept personal responsibility. This method permits the member to allow essentials to emerge rather than the leader having to prod the member to focus on the issue rathern than becoming mired in details.

## LEADING EXPRESSIVE PROCESSES

### Role of Theory

A group leader who wishes to use the expressive processes described in this book should be well versed in theory of psychological development, and in group leadership skills. These processes are designed to use group resources to help individuals work on issues/problems/concerns rather than as techniques for individuals. That is, a major emphasis is on group process.

Theory of psychological growth and development is fundamental in the preparation of group leaders who use expressive processes. No one theory is emphasized in this book, and the assumption is that these processes can be beneficial within any theoretical framework, but the group leader needs to have a solid basis from which to work. A theoretical framework provides the philosophical basis that leads to basic assumptions about the nature of humans and how they grow and develop. Theory also provides the basis for choosing when, how, and whether to intervene. The fundamentals of theory determine how these expressive processes will be used.

## GROUP LEADERSHIP SKILLS

### Linking

There are also basic group leadership skills the leader should possess: linking, blocking, observation, listening, and use of process. Linking is very necessary when using the resources of the group to help individuals. The leader has a responsibility to help members recognize similarities among themselves so that the group therapeutic factor of universality can emerge. Expressive processes often permit members to realize the extent of similarities on a deeper level without each member's having to have encountered the same situation or event. Since group members may get caught up in intense emotions, it is the responsibility of the group leader to link these similarities and point them out to members. Another situation where linking is important occurs when group members cannot see the patterns in their lives. Expressive processes can highlight these patterns, and the group leader's ability to link up disparate parts of self for the member is beneficial.

### Blocking

Blocking is a group leadership skill that is even more necessary when using expressive processes because members don't always recognize the intensity of emotions that are being experienced by self and others. This unawareness leads to inappropriate comments, questions, and advice-giving-all of which need to be blocked before they dilute or destroy the experience. A group leader must learn to block in such a way that neither the member who is acting inappropriately, nor the receiver is made to feel shamed or that he or she was "wrong." Blocking is a skill that involves sensitivity to emotional states, tact, and careful phrasing of the intervention.

### Observation

Careful observation allows the leader to identify resistances, when a member may be experiencing overwhelming emotional intensity, when members are uninvolved, or when there is increased anxiety. Deepening an experience, adjusting the intensity, and even rescuing members are all interventions that are dependent on observational skills of the leader. Understanding what is happening between members and within the group is very important for group progress in addition to helping individual members and allows an opportunity for group level interventions to be made by the leader. Attention to both verbal and nonverbal communication provides the leader with needed information. Observational skills are discussed more fully in the chapter on nonverbal communication.

### Listening

Listening also involves responding appropriately. It is probably the most important skill in the counselor's group of skills, and helps him or her make more appropriate interventions. Listening involves hearing the words, understanding their meanings and, most importantly, hearing the metacommunication. It is estimated that the majority of any communication is the nonverbal portion, and listening pays particular attention to this part. Further, it is very beneficial to the therapeutic process when group members feel heard and understood. It is not enough for the group leader to hear and understand: he/she must also convey the level and depth of his or her understanding to the member(s). This is the responding portion of listening.

### Use of Process

Effective use of group process demands that the group leader be able to tune into the process, make understanding comments about the process, and become adept at mass group commentary. *Group process* is the nature of the relationship that is taking place in the here and now between group members. *Process commentary* is making evident through verbalizations the extent, level, depth, and quality of the relationship that is being observed. *Mass group commentary* involves understanding what the group-as-a-whole is doing, and reporting on the observations to the group. These are skills learned over time and must be practiced. For more information on process commentary, consult Yalom's *The Theory and Practice of Group Psychotherapy* 3rd edition (1985).

## CROSS-CULTURAL CONSIDERATIONS

Race, ethnicity, and class variables influence group processes and outcomes. Their impact and influence are not well understood, nor are there delineated ways of making constructive use of them. The best information to date focuses on awareness of cultural variables that may cause misunderstandings and mis-communications. An expectation is that the group leader will have enough awareness and skill so that barriers and blunders due to cross-cultural variables will be minimized. The reader of this book is encouraged to read more on these topics than can be presented in this short discussion. A group leader is also expected to have a heightened awareness of his or her own cultural values and the impact of these values on his or her development and worldview.

## COMMON CROSS CULTURAL MISTAKES

### Highlighting Differences

There are four categories of common cross-cultural mistakes that can impair the development of a therapeutic relationship: highlighting of differences, insensitivity and ignorance, unawareness of communication barriers, and use of language. One of the most valued group therapeutic factors is universality, which highlights similarities among group members. Agazarian (1992) points out that subgroups form around similarities and dissolve around differences. Thus, highlighting cultural differences may have the effect of making people feel excluded even when the intent is to let them know they are valued for their difference(s). If it becomes necessary to focus on a cultural difference it should be done in such a way as to emphasize those similarities between members, and not highlight their differences. Diversity can be enriching when used properly, particularly when there is an attitude of wanting to understand the other in a nonjudgmental way. All too often the "different" member is made to feel that the difference is somehow unacceptable or wrong. Care must also be taken to insure that the "different" group member is not expected to contain all of the unwanted or uncomfortable emotions for the group.

### Insensitivity and Ignorance

Other common mistakes are insensitivity and ignorance. A group leader cannot be so knowledgeable as to eliminate the possibility of insensitivity and ignorance. Indeed, these crop up in the most intimate of relationships. However, it is the group leader's responsibility to become culturally knowledgeable about members in the group, and to block members' culturally offensive behaviors that are due to ignorancc. Cultural sensitivity and stages of development are described later. The most important point is that group leaders need to understand the significance of cross-cultural sensitivity.

### Communication Barriers

We are very much aware of communication barriers affecting understanding and relationships between people who know each other very well. Barriers such as hidden agendas, defensiveness, emotional blocks, and past experiences help to distort how and what messages are sent and received. These barriers may be exacerbated by cultural differences. For example, it is expected in the United States of America that when you do not understand or disagree with the teacher or group leader, that you can express this to him or her directly. In other cultures this behavior is unacceptable and rude. If a group leader has a group member from one of those cultural backgrounds and is not aware of the cultural communication barrier, he or she may draw the wrong conclusions. Gender and status differences may also play an important role in cross-cultural communication barriers.

### Language and Thought

Porter and Samovar (1991) define language as the "oral transmission of beliefs, values, norms and worldview." They go on to propose that language reveals *patterns of thought*: mental processes, forms of reasoning, and approaches to problem-solving. This definition suggests that a great deal is revealed through the use of language. Berman (1982) considers that *language* is used to "create pictures inside our heads that may or may not conform to the world of reality" and that "meanings are not in words, they are inside of people." There are numerous other definitions of language but all present the possibility that misunderstanding may arise as a result of language use. These misunderstandings happen within cultures where people have the same language and backgrounds. For example, confusion about meaning can arise from the use of "this" and "next" when referring to a weekend. For some, this weekend is the upcoming one, while for others the upcoming weekend is the "next" one and "this weekend" is the previous weekend. It's gotten to the point where I am careful to ask for the date when discussing weekends or say things like "this past weekend." There are many other examples of how use of simple words can convey different meanings to people who know and understand each other very well. It is very easy to see that language use with those from differing cultures can lead to confusion and misunderstandings.

### Jargon Free Language

In order to forestall some of the mistakes that language can cause, the group leader can use language that is as free from jargon as possible. This includes current jargon used in the wider culture. For example, a popular term used by many recently is "dis." It was even used in magazines such as *Newsweek*. It took considerable effort to find out what the definition was as none of my colleagues or graduate students with whom I work was able to give me a definition. If I had used it in group, there is the possibility that none of the members would have understood me. Another tactic would be to check with all group members continually on their understandings of what was said and/or meant. This is a good technique for group leaders to use even when group members appear to have similar cultural backgrounds, but is it essential when they do not.

## CULTURAL FACTORS AND RELATIONSHIPS

There are five major cultural factors that can affect relationships and lead to costly blunders: perception of time, individualism versus collectivism, use of space, role orderliness and conformity, and patterns of communication. Most of these factors are internalized and responded to on an unconscious level, *including that of the group leader.*

### Time

We in the United States tend to be more precise about appointments and schedules than people from some other cultures. We also expect that agreed-upon commitments for meeting, beginning a session, and so forth, will be kept, and may get upset when others appear to be careless about keeping to the agreement. Having an understanding about a particular culture's perception of time can prevent misunderstandings, and when a group leader has members from a different culture, he/she should make this one of the points in the study of the culture. One example of how perception of time could affect the therapeutic relationship is our usual expectation that when a question is posed, the receiver is to respond immediately. Some cultures do not have this expectation and a response may be given weeks later.

### I Versus We

Some cultures, such as the Japanese, have traditionally emphasized collectivism over individualism. This emphasis makes it difficult, if not impossible, for one person to express open disagreement with the group's position. Decisions are arrived at after all have had input and a consensus has been achieved. This orientation can be misleading to a group leader who is not aware of its importance for the group member's culture as he/she may take silence for consent and/or agreement for commitment. We in the United States especially in the mainstream, expect the individual to speak for him or herself directly and not to keep silent when he/she disagrees. We can accept that dependency issues may influence the individual's capacity to do so, but may overlook cultural determinants.

### Space

Use of space is a very important factor because invasion of personal space is very uncomfortable and anxiety producing. Invasion can cause physiological reactions such as rapid heartbeat and a surge of adrenaline to prepare the body for fight or flight. The personal zone is culturally determined and is an indication of the status of the individual. In the Western world the following guidelines are used:

Intimate zone-six to eighteen inches

Personal zone-eighteen inches to four feet (social functions, friendly gatherings)

Social zone-four to twelve feet (comfort zone for strangers of others who enter our space, such as the plumber)

Public zone-over twelve feet

These guidelines are suggestions, and group leaders are encouraged to understand group members' use of space regardless of cultural background. The use of space also involves use of touch, for one has to invade the intimate zone in order to touch. Knowing the group member's tolerance for others entering his or her intimate zone may signal whether touch will be threatening.

### Status

Role orderliness and conformity refer to status. In some cultures the status or role for members has a set of rigid guidelines for behavior that must not be violated. For example, in some Middle Eastern countries doing any work with the hands, such as fixing a machine, is considered demeaning, and only those from the servant class are expected to "work with their hands." In the United States we have quite a different perception which can lead to misunderstandings if cultural differences are not known. Our roles and status are much more flexible than those in many parts of the world and group leaders need to be aware of expectations in order not to be confusing to members or to give offense. Ignorance may also lead the group leader to fail to show expected respect, which, in turn, influences development of the therapeutic relationship.

### Patterns of Communication

Patterns of communication can also present opportunities for misunderstandings and blunders when cultural differences are influential. *Patterns* refer to who initiates dialogue, to whom it is directed, who supports whom, deference to others, agreement and disagreement, and silence. These are all behaviors that are routinely observed by the group leader but, if not observed with cultural determinants in mind, can lead to errors about what is happening in the group, and with individual group members. For example, silence may not be resistance from a member whose culture demands that they show deference to authority figures, such as the gorup leader. Silence, in this instance, may be their way of showing respect and deference instead of openly verbalizing disagreement with something the leader said.

## STEPS THE GROUP LEADER CAN TAKE

Developing cultural sensitivity occurs over time but can be assisted. One step is to consult resources about the culture. There are usually numerous books and articles on the cultural factors that have implications for the therapeutic relationship and interactions in the group. The following are other suggestions:

1. *Find a cultural mentor if possible.* Ideally, a mental health professional from the culture about which you are interested would be most in tune with factors that are most important.

2. *Withhold judgment.* Other cultures may have traditions and practices that are at odds with those common in the United States. It is impossible to know whether a group member has totally accepted the traditional practices, modified them, or rejected them. You also do not know what impact these practices and traditions have or will have on the process of group counseling. Keeping an open mind helps facilitate acceptance, respect, and regard for group members from that culture.

3. *Recognize when you experience negative feelings about the culture.* Expect conflicts between your beliefs, values, and so on, and those of people from another culture. Some may even threaten your basic values and arouse intensely negative feelings. These conflicts are more apt to be worked through and resolved in some way if you acknowledge and accept them. Your acknowledgment of negative feelings can also

help you take precautions to prevent them from impeding the therapeutic relationship and group progress. It is possible to be nonjudgmental, respectful, and accepting of individuals from cultures that arouse negative feelings in you.

4. *Cultivate flexibility and patience with yourself and with others.* It takes time to develop knowledge and sensitivity to other cultures, and sometimes you may feel that you will never understand. You may also have group members you feel will never understand our culture no matter how long they live in the United States, or how many generations have lived here. Both you and they have probably made considerable progress and are continuing to work on it.

## Phases of Development of Cultural Sensitivity

Acuff (1993) lists four phases of cultural development: *excitement*, awakening, disillusionment, and realization. After accepting the challenge of learning about a new culture most people have a sense of excitement and anxiety. They are eager to learn and tend to immerse themselves in reading and talking with knowledgeable others about that culture. There is usually the attitude or assumption that people all over the world are basically the same and with a little effort they can be understood.

The second phase--*awakening*--generally occurs when you realize that there are deep cultural differences that are annoying, or even offensive. These may be somewhat minor, such as arrival on time for appointments, or major annoyances such as the perception and valuing of females. This phase is also a reality check; differences are important. The group leader should also realize that these cultural differences may make a difference to the member's capacity to relate to the leader and to other group members. It is also important in this phase to continue to reflect on similarities.

Phase three--*disillusionment*--occurs when you begin to feel overwhelmed by the degree and depth of the differences. There may be many that conflict with your basic values, and you may feel that your values are too fundamental to allow you to be accepting of conflicting ones. People from other cultures begin to feel "alien" to you, and you may even lose sight of the assumption you began with that "people all over the world are basically the same." Accepting this phase and realizing that it is a step to the next one can help minimize the extent of this phase, and any possible negative impact.

The final phase--*accepting*--occurs when you accept what can and cannot be accomplished. That is, there are some differences that cannot be satisfactorily solved but must be resolved to some degree. It helps if you can accept that which seems reasonable to you of the other culture, stay somewhat neutral about a position, and let go of the rest kind of agreeing to disagree. One way of going about this is to determine which factors affect the relationship and/or progress and to work on these: let the rest go.

# 2

# MAXIMIZING OUTCOMES

## GUIDE FOR ENHANCING EXPRESSIVE PROCESSES

### Expected Benefits

Both the counselor and group members can expect to realize benefits from using expressive processes. The counselor will find the counseling process to be enhanced and expanded, and group members can expect progress toward their individual therapeutic goals. There is one other entity that can experience a payoff--the group itself. Many times group progress and process are enriched, and that promotes therapeutic development and healing. It is very important that expressive processes be used to further therapeutic goals and not serve as mere techniques.

The group leader has special responsibilities that, when realized, lead to positive outcomes. These responsibilities fall into two categories; therapeutic attitude and skills. Group members also have responsibilities. They can expect to gain more from expressive processes if they are willing to participate, self-disclose, be open to expressing whatever feelings or emotions arise, and seek to be genuine and honest with self and others.

### Leader Responsibilities

The therapeutic attitude of the group leader plays an important role in encouraging participation and deriving personal growth in group. *Attitude* refers to "a position of the body assumed consciously or unconsciously, and, by extension, to mental outlook" (Funk and Wagnall, 1963 p. 94). This definition reflects both an inner and an external position and, when used to denote a therapeutic *attitude,* indicate that the self-hood of the counselor plays a major role and, that this "attitude" is conveyed both verbally and nonverbally. Berne (1973) considers a therapeutic attitude to have the following components: the physical condition of the therapist, the psychological attitude, the therapeutic relationship, the therapist's assets, and observational and listening skills. This discussion builds on those components and adds others: a here and now focus, ethical considerations, and cross-cultural sensitivity.

### Physical Condition

It is difficult to be fully present when one is sick or not feeling up to par. Paying attention becomes an effort; if ears are congested, listening is impaired; pain is distracting; and on and on. While it is possible to lead a productive group session, there is always the possibility that more significant clues will be missed than usual, assuming that even the expert group leader misses something of importance sometimes. However, not being in top physical condition should be an indication to the group leader to try to be more alert even though he/she is not feeling well.

Leading a group takes stamina, and expressive processes demand even more energy. Most are very simple to initiate, however, considerable important material can emerge and must be dealt with immediately. It is not wise to try to carry over important and significant feelings until the next session because some members may not have adequate coping resources to handle these anxiety provoking feelings and emotions. Therefore, the group leader must have enough physical resources to carry the process through to a satisfactory resolution or point.

### Psychological Attitude

In this discussion *psychological attitude* focuses on concern and caring for others. Included are also knowledge of human growth and development, as well as emotional and psychological disabling conditions; belief in group and expressive processes; and willingness to engage in self-development. A group leader leads by example as well as by skills. What a group leader is appears to be more important than what he/she does, although actions are influenced by beliefs, attitudes, and values. A group leader has the responsibility to understand basic principles of human growth and development and be well grounded in theory of psychological development. The leader must convey belief in group and expressive processes if members are to get anything that is therapeutically useful out of them. Belief that members can benefit encourages participation and self-exploration.

### A Therapeutic Relationship

Developing a therapeutic relationship is crucial for positive outcomes. It is through the therapeutic relationship that group members become willing to trust, self-disclose, and let their true self be known or revealed. There are certain basic skills and characteristics that have been shown to enhance development of a therapeutic relationship. Skills such as concreteness, immediacy, confrontation, attending, listening and responding, and appropriate self-disclosure appear to be important. Characteristics such as genuineness, warmth and caring, respect for the uniqueness of others and a nonjudgmental attitude are all important.

One of the most important things for a group leader to remember is that a therapeutic relationship develops over time and is gradual. Members have to learn to trust the leader and this trust must be earned. It is not easily given, nor is it automatic. Therefore, learning and practicing basic skills are important because they help convey to members those personal characteristics that enhance the therapeutic relationship, promote trust and feelings of safety, and convey the leader's belief in the efficacy of group.

### Leader Assets

The primary assets that a group leader must possess are a high degree of self-knowledge and group leadership skills. Knowing oneself is crucial to prevent countertransference blunders. The group leader has a responsibility to prevent countertransference issues from impeding and/or influencing the group progress, and this is best accomplished by self-knowledge of one's own issues, concerns, problems. It is also important because one of the best sources of information about what is happening in the group resides in the experiencing of the group leader. The ability to access one's current experiencing, understand it, and use the information constructively demands a high level of expertise but is one of the best assets a group leader can have. Developing this ability promotes group and individual progress toward therapeutic goals.

### Leader Skills

Group leadership skills such as linking, enhancing strengths, focusing the group on process rather than content, blocking destructive or unproductive behaviors, helping members make contact with inner feelings, providing constructive feedback, and modeling desired behaviors are also assets the leader can cultivate to advantage. Many, if not most, of these skills are used in individual and family counseling also. However, some are used differently in groups. For example, linking to emphasize similarities between members promotes universality, which is an important therapeutic factor. When used in individual counseling it usually connects similarities in events, attitudes, and so on, for one person so that patterns become more evident.

Observational and listening skills are discussed more fully under nonverbal communication. These skills also impact the development of a therapeutic relationship between the leader and group members. They complement the leader characteristics of genuineness, warmth, positive regard and caring. The most important points to remember are that observations should be a source of information to promote understanding for the group leader and do not necessarily need to be openly reported or commented on, and that it is important that members feel listened to and heard. Both observation and listening demand and imply a focus on unspoken feelings and emotions as these are the major and most accurate parts of communication. The other side is that group members are observing and listening to the leader also, so that whatever is being conveyed to them should be authentic and genuine.

### Here-and-Now Focus

Expressive processes seem to be most useful if there is a here-and-now focus. Past events can be reexperienced this way, allowing residual feelings and emotions to emerge and enhancing the likelihood of their being dealt with constructively. When processing an exercise it is all too easy to fall into the trap of story telling. A lot of material, usually painful, emerges rapidly and the individual tries to communicate all details. If you notice, as he/she talks more about what emerged, the person begins to distance and emotionally detach him or herself more. On one hand, this movement away from the emotional content helps control it better. On the other hand, the opportunity is lost to experience the emotional content safely *and* begin to deal with it. Keeping the focus on here-and-now experiencing demonstrates to members that the group is a safe place to experience or re-experience emotionally laden material *and* be guided in dealing with it in ways that can lead to solutions or resolutions. The group leader maintains a here-and-now focus by structuring the process to be present-centered: gently guiding members to allow awareness of the experience to be felt, bringing the discussion back from there and then, blocking story telling, and heading off intellectualizing.

## ETHICAL CONSIDERATIONS

Group leaders must be knowledgeable about ethical principles for group work. These ethical principles are contained in codes and guidelines for all mental health professionals and licensure or certification requirements. Major ethical considerations when using expressive processes include "do no harm," informed consent, personal problems and conflicts, misuse of influence, competence and appropriate use, privacy and confidentiality, and maintaining of expertise.

### Prevention of Harm

"Do no harm" refers to taking reasonable precautions to ensure that members are not damaged psychologically. This means having an adequate knowledge of the level of emotional maturity and functioning, capacity to tolerate anxiety, and stability of group members before introducing an expressive process. The leader would also want to take care not to offend cultural, social, or religious sensibilities. For example, guided imagery is viewed by some as being a "tool of the devil" or an attempt at mind control. While the leader does not perceive imagery in this way, research has shown it to be useful in helping individuals cope with physical illnesses, and the proposed purpose is to benefit the group member; nevertheless its use should be reviewed for potential harm.

### Informed Consent

Informed consent has two components: The first is telling members what the exercise or activity will be, the looked-for outcome(s), and the likely benefit/risks for members. The second part is obtaining their consent. Members should be given enough information about the proposed expressive process so that they can evaluate the personal risk. The group leader should *describe the structure of the activity*: "I'm going to ask you to draw some symbols you associate with certain emotions"; *state the goal or purpose*: "This exercise is designed to get you thinking about those emotions that are easy for you to express and those that are difficult, and help the group begin to see similarities"; and *prepare members for any potential risk(s)*: "Most people find this an easy and enjoyable exercise to do but sometimes, a very painful association emerges. If this happens, we stop the exercise to help deal with the emotion." Requesting consent could be worded thus, "Given this description, is this an exercise you're willing to try?" Survey each group member and, if there is opposition or significant reluctance, explore the resistance and discard the activity. You will probably get more out of addressing the resistance than out of using the exercise. Other benefits are; members become empowered, feel more in control, trust you to be sensitive to their concerns, are more likely to participate in future expressive activities, and you learn something about the feasibility of using this particular exercise.

### Personal Issues of Leader

The leader's personal problems and conflicts; that is countertransference, will interfere with the effectiveness of the group and pose potential harm to group members. Group leaders need to have a heightened awareness of their personal issues, have worked on them, seek professional consultation or assistance when appropriate, and evaluate each expressive process for possible conflicts. The potential for countertransference is high when the leader has not worked through personal problems and conflicts and/or is not aware of them. This is one reason why participation as a group member is important in the process and training to become a group leader.

### Use of Influence

A group leader has the ethical responsibility not to misuse his or her influence with group members. Members tend to idealize the leader in some ways, and see him or her as "the expert." The leader is perceived as very powerful, and in some instances, such as court ordered counseling, may be very powerful. It is very important that the group leader not misuse this influence to manipulate members into participating in an activity even if the leader feels the outcomes would be positive, and there is little or no risk involved. Members should freely choose to participate. Empowering members to make decisions about participating also demonstrates faith in their capacity to make choices that are in their best interest.

### Appropriateness of Techniques

*Competence and appropriate use* refer to the expertise of the group leader to use the particular expressive process. Many of those described in the book are relatively easy to implement. However, structuring exercises and processing them to maximize potential positive impact for group members require that the leader be knowledgeable about process commentary; understand how to set up the particular kind of exercise, such as art; and have some personal experience with the medium. It is most useful, and recommended, that the leader have some instruction in the process. This background will increase the likelihood that exercises will be used appropriately.

### Confidentiality

It is assumed that the issue of confidentiality would have been explored and specified for the group prior to initiating an expressive process. Because sensitive, personal material is likely to emerge from an exercise it may be useful to remind members of the extent of confidentiality. The group leader must also keep in mind the need to respect the confidentiality rights of group members when writing reports, consulting, and so forth. Only information that is germane to the purpose should be shared, and that only with the appropriate professional(s) or persons concerned. Members are more likely to want to participate in expressive processes that explore sensitive material if they can rely on the leader and other members to maintain confidentiality.

### Developing and Maintaining Expertise

Expressive processes continue to evolve and develop, necessitating that those who use them maintain expertise in the area. It is the group leader's responsibility to continue to read studies and articles on these processes; attend conferences, workshops, demonstrations, or classes; and continue to develop knowledge and skill in all aspects.

## GROUP MEMBERS RESPONSIBILITIES

Group members also have some responsibilities and attitudes that help maximize payoffs for them from expressive processes: willingness to participate, self-awareness and self-disclosure, and honesty with self and others. The ethical issue of maintaining confidentiality refers to group members also.

### Participation

Willingness to participate on more than a superficial level involves some degree of psychological risk. For example, the group member risks remembering repressed and/or denied material that has been defended against to protect the "self." Most often this is very painful, even shameful material that affects how the individual perceives him or herself. Material that emerges put the member at the risk of understanding his or her self-defeating behavior, or seeing patterns of destruction in self and others. While the process of counseling or therapy seeks to uncover this material so that the person can begin to work through it for resolution or solution, expressive processes can accelerate the unfolding process and, in so doing, present the person with painful, anxiety-producing material. Many group members sense this risk and limit their participation to a superficial level. Others participate, peeling away a layer at a time. All participation involves a certain amount of trust in the group leader, group process, and other group members. It takes time for this trust to develop to the point where the individual is knowingly willing to risk having this material emerge. The group leader can encourage members to participate and try the exercise on whatever level is comfortable for them, and empower them to decide for themselves.

### Present Centeredness and Expression

Members can get more personal benefit from expressive processes if they learn to be more aware of current experiencing *and* be willing to report their awareness and experiencing. The group leader can guide the awareness by having members focus on what they are experiencing, such as bodily tension, feelings, emotions, associations, or triggered memories. If they follow the guiding and allow themselves to become more aware, the next step is to disclose to the group. Disclosure appears to legitimize the experience and promote acceptance of it by the individual, and it can be the beginning of the working through process. The leader needs to be alert to suppression of feelings and emotions aroused by the exercise and encourage those members to express some of what they have experienced. Attention to nonverbal behavior provides cues for the leader. I like to check in with all members and do so if they do not volunteer to disclose. Asking each member in turn to report on what the experience was like for him or her, or what was easy, or what was hard is usually enough to get members talking about the experience. If the group has been together long enough and a therapeutic relationship established, the leader may want to address reluctance to disclose directly by telling the member what he/she observed (e.g., tears that were not shed) and expressing concern that he/she, the leader, wants to make sure the member is not sitting on intense feelings that could be engulfing after the session. The leader will want to make sure members can handle emergent feelings and emotions outside the group, and members have a responsibility to disclose these feelings *even though they do not feel them to be troublesome.*

### Authenticity

It will be difficult for members to be honest with themselves. It is difficult for anyone. However, if they will make an attempt to be honest and genuine with themselves, they will reap significant benefits. Knowledge about self, insight, easier decisions, awarenesses and problem resolution are all possible benefits. Total honesty may not be possible, but any level of honesty facilitates counseling.

Honesty with others can help, also, but must be tempered with tact and an awareness of the emotional state of the other: that is, will it help, are members able to accept and use it, can they tolerate it? Members need to learn how to give constructive, honest feedback that helps the other person. Giving and receiving honest feedback in a group are valuable resources that are not usually available in other settings.

## FEEDBACK GUIDELINES

Group leaders can facilitate awareness, insight, learning, and understanding for members by responding in a manner that relies on nonintrusive feedback rather than interpretation or analysis. A major purpose for using expressive processes should be to aid group members to derive their own meanings for the experience and not have someone else's meaning imposed, either the leader's or other group members'. This is not to say that others' interpretation or analysis has no value or validity. It may be completely accurate. However, there is considerable risk that the interpretation or analysis may be too much for the person to handle at that time and he/she feels overwhelmed, shutting down (resisting) or, worse, giving in to the engulfing feelings. The following guidelines are intended to facilitate group members' acceptance of and working with the material that emerges.

### Be Aware of Emotional State

The group leader needs to be aware of the emotional states of group members during and after the expressive experience. Careful observation of nonverbal behaviors is most useful in determining this, with verbalizations as a follow-up source of information. Noting the depth of emotional involvement provides clues as to the amount and level of feedback they could accept and use. Sometimes the most useful counselor intervention is just to let the member vent or talk, giving little or no verbal response--but using a lot of positive nonverbal communication. At other times paraphrasing what the member is verbalizing to provide a sharper, clear focus of the emotional content is needed. At still other times, or for other members, feedback that deepens the experience is useful. The counselor needs to be sensitive to the varying emotional states of members and gauge responses accordingly.

### Temper the Amount

Provide the amount of information the member(s) can use, not the amount you want to give. Information is most useful if it is not overwhelming. If members feel engulfed by the amount of information given by the leader, they tend to pull back and are able to use very little or none of it. It is probably better to give too little information rather than too much. Remember that members will experience intense emotions from many of the expressive processes, and, while they are under the influence of these intense emotions, they are unable to process a lot of information. Use observation and listening skills to monitor the reactions as a guide for stopping or continuing to give members information.

The amount may also need to be adjusted because of the "coat-tailing" phenomenon. While the leader is interacting with or providing feedback to one member, others are following, and it may be difficult to gauge just how emotionally involved other members are. When it appears that the process is deepening for one member, the leader may need to check other members to assess their tolerance for continuing. Doing less than one wants is infinitely better than doing too much, especially if the too much is for a member that hides it successfully.

### Clarifying the Feedback or Communication

The leader needs to make sure that members understand what was meant by what was said. Even in the best of times or situations meanings are subject to many interpretations depending on the individual. When emotional turmoil is added to the communication conditions become ripe for misunderstandings. On the other hand, clarification should not degenerate into an intellectual discussion over meanings. The best method for clarifying is to have receivers of feedback rephrase what they thought they heard.

### Consequences of Feedback

Pay close attention to the impact of the leader's feedback. What effect is it having on the member? Increasing the anxiety? Decreasing the anxiety? Puzzling? Promoting reflection? Causing the member to retreat, withdraw, or shut down? The impact tells you whether to continue, stop, modify, or whether clarification is needed. Again, the best indicator is nonverbal behavior. This attention should also be extended to other group members. If you are uncertain of the impact for the feedback, ask members if they are anxious, need more clarification, or would like an opportunity to reflect on what has been said.

### Descriptive, Specific, Behavioral

Describe what was done, said, or observed without adding why it was done or said. Why gets into interpretation and analysis, and that should be avoided. Whys are also based on assumptions and inferences and these may cause resistance rather than promoting self-exploration.

The leader should be specific rather than general. General statements often lead to misinterpretations, or an extended intellectual discussion about meanings. For example, when a member is told that he/she was, or seemed to be resisting, much time and effort go into clarifying or overcoming the natural defensiveness that is aroused when one is told he/she is "resisting." The person may very well have been resisting but are not about to accept or admit it. The member is more likely to accept a statement that points out what he/she was saying or doing and what the effect was for the leader.

Observable behavior is generally more acceptable when giving feedback. Even when individuals are not aware of their behavior they are more likely to accept observations because these are easily verified by others. It is important to point out significant behaviors rather than interpretations, for interpretations are subject to misunderstandings and/or error while behavior is an observable event.

**Leave Space**

Give members the freedom to accept and decide for themselves the value and/or validity of the feedback. Do not impose ideas, opinions, or advice. Allow enough space so that members are empowered. They may not be ready to accept the level and/or depth of self-knowledge, awareness, insight, or understanding at this time. However, it is most likely that they will return to it at some future time, particularly if it is their choice and the group leader has shown confidence in their ability to handle it.

# 3

# NONVERBAL COMMUNICATION

## RATIONALE, IMPORTANCE AND PURPOSES

### Introduction

It would be difficult to overestimate the importance of understanding nonverbal communication in the therapeutic process. Indeed, it has been suggested that the greatest part of messages is communicated nonverbally. For example, Kline and Johannsen (1935) noted that the face is the primary way to identify the nature of the emotional response, and Mehrabian (1971) found that facial expressions were believed when words and expressions were inconsistent. Thus, it is important for the counselor to be aware of his or her own nonverbal communication, and to tune into and understand the nonverbal communication of clients.

### Purposes

There are six purposes for messages sent or portrayed nonverbally: repeating, contradicting, substituting, complementing, accenting, and regulating (Mader and Mader, 1990). The purpose of the message lies within the individual; this means that the receiver must interpret the purpose in order to understand the message. It takes practice and keen observational skills to become adept and accurate in interpreting the purpose of an individual's nonverbal communication.

### Repeating

Nonverbal repeating means that the nonverbal behavior is congruent with verbalizations and serves to reinforce them. For example, someone says that he/she is upset and cries. One does not have to guess the purpose of the tears: they have been clearly and directly expressed.

### Congruence

When nonverbal behaviors are incongruent with verbalizations they are termed contradictory. This is a signal that the person may not be in touch with his or her emotions, and is denying their existence, or in some way, resisting. An example of incongruent nonverbal behavior is when someone denies that he/she is angry but has clenched their fists, tensed the body, and has a facial expression that indicates strong emotion. Another example someone who says that an event did not upset him or her but is wringing his or her hands.

### Substituting

Substituting refers to using a gesture to communicate without words. Examples are using a wave for goodbyes, smiles instead of greetings, and the "finger" to indicate displeasure. These are usually culturally determined and, in some instances, regionally determined. Thus, a gesture may be lost or misunderstood if the receiver is from a different region/place than the sender.

### Accenting

Accenting is used to intensify the verbal message. Tone of voice and gestures add emphasis to words, leading the receiver to take the sender's intent more seriously. Sometimes it is difficult to convey the intensity of feeling through words and accenting becomes a more accurate indicator for the message. Some examples are opening eyes wide, rounding the mouth, putting hands to face to intensify surprise, clenching teeth, balling up hands into fists, and moving into the other's personal space to intensify anger.

### Influence

Nonverbal gestures can also be used to regulate, control, and influence the behavior or responses of others. Frowning to indicate displeasure by a parent usually brings about changes in the child's behavior. Most of us are familiar with "that look" given us by a parent that indicated that we had better stop doing whatever we were doing. A finger on the lips to indicate that we wish someone to be quieter, a finger drawn across the throat to say that it is time to stop talking, and waving of a hand to ask someone to join you are all examples of nonverbal gestures as regulators. The power of the leader's nonverbal gestures is very influential in the group and leaders must be aware of their nonverbel behaviors as well as observing that of members.

### Social Functions of Nonverbal Communication

Mader and Mader (1990) describe the social functions of nonverbal communications as cognitive processing and learning, expressive communication, impression formation and management, relational communication, deception, and structuring and regulating of interactions. Understanding these functions aids in accurately interpreting the nonverbal communication of others.

### Cognitive

*Cognitive processing* and *learning* refer to observing the nonverbal communication of an individual in the context of verbal behavior, deriving accurate meanings and understandings from the observation, and using the knowledge in future interactions. The same word or words can be used to convey different meanings. For example, the word *marvelous* when used with a sarcastic intonation, a frown or grimace, and shrugging of the shoulders convey a meaning different from when it is accompanied by a smile of pleasure, an upbeat voice tone, and opening or spreading of arms. Becoming aware that the individual is using the same word with differing nonverbal gestures, and then using the information to respond accurately to him or her in future interactions is an example of cognitive processing and learning.

### Expressive

*Expressive communication* occurs when we indicate what we are feeling nonverbally. This assumes an awareness of inner experiencing, a willingness to allow others to see our feelings and emotions, and an appropriate mechanism for expressing them. While it is possible for there to be an unconscious nonverbal communication of inner experiencing, this function, used in a social way, tends to rely more on a conscious awareness of feelings and emotions. That is, we intend to express these particular feelings and emotions. We are willing to allow someone else to see us as we are, and we have the means to express these feelings appropriately.

### Impressions

Nonverbal communication can be used to convey an impression of self that is intended to convince others of the kind of person one is or wishes to be. Nonverbal cues are used often to determine how one is perceived. Cues such as physical appearance, gender, age, dress, movement, and voice are used to judge ethnicity, social and economic status, and geographical origin. Other nonverbal cues are associated with social attitudes, values, and acceptability of others. If one wants to join or be considered part of a particular group, then his or her nonverbal communication should be similar to the group's in order to convey the impressing that he/she is "one of them."

### Relationships

Nonverbal communication behaviors tell much about the relationship between people. These behaviors are used to create, maintain, and change relationships regardless of the degree of intimacy in the relationship. That is, casual relationships are just as much defined by nonverbal communication behaviors as are more intimate relationships. For example, it is said that a love affair between two people is as hard to conceal as a case of measles. This is because the extent and level of the relationship is clear to others by the nonverbal behaviors. A song notes that people are talking because the two stand a little too close, hold a gaze just a little too long, and smile at each other a lot.

### Deception

Nonverbal messages tend to be somewhat ambiguous; this allows them to be exploited by those whose intent is to deceive. Not all uses to deceive are wrong or bad. There are instances where it is in the best interest of the individual that his or her real feelings not be apparent. For example, when receiving a dressing down from the boss, or being challenged by the police, and participating in a hostile meeting are situations where someone's being able to read your feelings puts you at a disadvantage. However, there are times when the intent of the nonverbal message is to deceive in order to take advantage of someone else. The salesperson who has an open posture, smiles, turns his/her palms up with arms spread to convey "trust," and is lying is using nonverbal gestures to deceive. The individual who looks you directly in the eye with a steady gaze and lies is another example. The television character Fred Sanford, using his fake heart attack--"This is the big one"--in order to get his way or manipulate others, is another example.

### Structuring and Regulating

The final social function is structuring and regulating interaction by defining the situation and the relationship(s) in it; regulating the amount, frequency, and nature of the conversation; and providing interactional synchronization. It is through nonverbal communication that one comes to understand the situation in which one is operating at the moment, the relationship of him or her to others in the same situation, and the rules of engagement. This particular function is discussed more fully in the chapter on structuring the group.

## CATEGORIES OF NONVERBAL BEHAVIORS

Categories of nonverbal behaviors that provide cues to the emotional content of messages and the "real" meaning are kinetics, facial expressions, expressive speech or voice-related behaviors, physiological responses, physical characteristics, and general appearance.

### Kinetics

*Kinetics* refers to use of the body in communicating. It includes posture, gestures, body movement, and touching. A group leader will find it useful to observe the posture of members in different positions, such as standing, walking, and sitting. From the moment the client approaches the counselor or walks into the room, his or her posture is telling much about the internal emotional state. For example, someone who enters a room slowly, tentatively, head pulled into neck with eyes down, and shoulders slumped is nonverbally projecting dejection. Another person might enter the room with the head up and back, stiff legs, shoulders back and straight, and an exaggerated swing of arms, thereby projecting self-satisfaction, maybe even pompousness.

Sitting postures also convey much about the individual. Warmth, cooperation, and interest are indicated by forward lean, eye contact, and close physical distance. The reverse of these postures indicates a more negative attitude. Clients or therapists who choose to straddle a chair convey an attitude of intent to dominate with the chair acting as a shield to protect from an attack. A leg thrown over the arm of a chair signals a lack of concern about the topic under discussion, a kind of indifference (Pease, 1984).

Standing, walking, and sitting postures convey information about territorial claims, dominance, and readiness. Leaning against someone or something extends your boundaries to incorporate the other person or thing, conveying "ownership." Doing so without permission from the other person, or on property or space that does not belong to you, is an attempt to intimidate or control. Doorway leaners are a good example of the attempt to intimidate or control nonverbally. On the other hand, a standing posture that is erect with palms visible tends to make a favorable impression. Standing erect, hands on hips with a slight forward lean conveys readiness.

## BODY MOVEMENTS

### Intimacy

A cue to the degree of intimacy between two or more people is the physical distance between them. The angle at which they orient their bodies is also reflective of their attitudes and relationship. Inclusion and exclusion can be determined by how group members orient their bodies. If bodies are not turned so as to include others, and only the head turns, then others are not being invited to join. Crossing the knees toward a person also indicates inclusion and acceptance.

### Tension

Body movements provide cues to the degree of relaxation or anxiety being experienced by group members. Usually, the more movement of body parts the less the relaxation, indicating increased anxiety. Sometimes, anxiety is masked and little movement occurs, however, there is considerable muscular tension--a kind of "holding in." Other movements to be observed include rocking movements of the body, head nodding, leg movements, and foot movements. Usually, the more frequent and consistent the movement, the more tension or anxiety is present. It is difficult to discuss body movements without discussing gestures as gestures also involve movement of legs, arms, and the head.

### Gestures

The first and most important thing to remember about understanding gestures is that the message is contained in a "cluster" of gestures and to not try to interpret a gesture in isolation. It is easy to be mistaken about the message of an individual gesture. Care must be taken to observe the cluster that occurs, or is sustained, over a period of time. Ruesch and Kees (1956) believe that gestures are used to illustrate, emphasize, point, explain, or interrupt and cannot be separated from verbal communication. Gestures expand and enhance verbal communications but can also be used in place of words. Some clusters of gestures that may be particularly useful for group leaders are those that indicate openness, defensiveness, readiness, need for reassurance, cooperation, frustration, confidence, nervousness, acceptance, and an attempt to control self. Table 3.1 presents examples of gestures clusters and corresponding messages. Table 3.2 presents some examples of gesture clusters for certain conditions for adults and adolescents.

### Facial Expressions

Expressions on the face are vital clues to the nature of emotional responses and provide much information on the current emotional state of the individual. Although many persons can "mask" their true feelings, the presence of a "mask" is then significant. That is, what do they fear from open expressions of their emotions, or are they able to get in touch with and be aware of what they are experiencing? Facial expressiveness is a critical party of the therapeutic process for both the client and the counselor. The client judges the extent to which he/she is valued, understood, cared for, accepted, and respected from expressions on the counselor's face. The counselor judges the extent of emotional distress, degree of resistance, avoidant behaviors, and comfort level by the client's facial expression. The focus on facial expressiveness as indicative of inner experiencing appears to be consistent across cultures. Ekman (1965) found that certain facial expressions, such as those indicating anger, fear, surprise, sadness, disgust, and happiness, are the same across cultures. What differs are the situations that provoke these emotions, the occasions where they will be displayed, *whether* they will be displayed or suppressed, and to what degree will they be displayed or suppressed. It is also important to be knowledgable of the impact of culture in determining what facial expressions are appropriate to display and which are not. Group members' facial expressions may need to be understood in the context of their culture.

Facial expressions are best observed as a whole rather than in isolation although there are certain parts of the face that tend to convey more information even in isolation. Lips and eyebrows are two examples. Raised eyebrows convey surprise, especially when accompanied by widening of the eyes. Raising one eyebrow while narrowing the eyes conveys skepticism. Lips move in smiles, frowns, and expressions of disgust. Smiles vary from the polite with little movement of the lips and none for the eyes, to that with lots of widening of lips and eyes.

Perhaps the most important thing for the counselor to notice is any shift or change in facial expression. The shift or change may be slight or fleeting but may contain much information about the emotional state of the client.

### Vocal Behaviors

The voice is also a nonverbal communication. That is, the tone (pitch, level, intensity) inflection, spacing of words, emphases, pauses, tempo, silences, and fluency also convey information--not just the words that are used.

**Table 3.1**
**Examples of Gesture Clusters and Corresponding Messages**

| Message | Gesture Cluster Examples |
|---|---|
| Acceptance | Forward lean, moving closer, eye contact, relaxed arms and hands |
| Confidence | Steepling fingers, using personal objects to extend territory, leaning back with hands supporting head, head up when walking |
| Cooperation | Tilted head, forward lean with feet flat on floor, arms and hands relaxed |
| Defensiveness | Arms closed on chest in a protective or fixed position, leg over arm of chair, straddling a chair, fists clenched |
| Frustration | Short breaths, tightly clenched hands with elbows on table, hand wringing, kicking the ground or an imaginary object |
| Nervousness | Clearing throat, fidgeting in chair, hand covering mouth |
| Openness | Forward lean, arms relaxed, fingers flat and extended, legs uncrossed |
| Readiness | Hands on hips while standing with forward lean, moving in, lowering voice, uncrossed legs when seated |
| Need for reassurance | Clenched hands, rubbing thumbs together, picking cuticles, pinching flesh on back of hand, pen or pencil in mouth, twirling hair, fondling necklace or earrings, bringing hand to throat slowly |

*Tone* refers to the pitch, level, and intensity of the vocalization. Raising the tone of voice is usually associated with annoyance, irritation, or alarm. Lowering the tone is associated with various emphases such as surprise, disappointment, or incredulity. Changes in tone are usually indicative of changes in affect.

Listening for inflection, spacing, emphases, and pauses provides clues to the group leader of the inner experiencing of group members. The leader can become aware of when the members are encountering a new awareness, achieving insight, retreating from sensitive and/or painful material, or resisting, or level of members' comfort. "Sitting on" significant emotions is often conveyed by these voice behaviors.

Listening for shifts and changes in speech tempo, silences, and fluency can also be beneficial. A speeded up tempo is usually associated with annoyance, anxiety, and so on, while a decreased tempo is associated with uncertainty. Much of what is to be observed and listened for is in relation to the individual's customary or usual vocal behavior.

Attitude of members and leader is conveyed primarily through vocal nonverbal behaviors. A positive attitude is associated with higher rates of speech, longer periods of talking, more use of gestures, and less disturbance of speech such as pauses, spacing, silence, pleasant facial expression, and frequent head nods. A negative attitude is associated with the reverse of these nonverbal behaviors.

**Table 3.2**
**Examples of Gesture Clusters as Indicators of Conditions for Adults and Adolescents**

| Condition | Usual Nonverbal Behaviors |
|---|---|
| Anxiety | Rapid, and/or restless movement of limbs, hand tremors, fidgeting, overcontrolled to the point of tension |
| Depression | Very slow movements; slumped, dejected posture, long pauses between words, lack of eye contact, sighs, hyperactivity |
| Isolation and Withdrawal | Arms kept in close contact with body, head lowered, lack of sustained eye contact, greater physical distance from others, talk very little |

## Physiological Nonverbal Behaviors

There are several observable autonomic physiological responses that communicate inner experiencing; for instance, blushing, paleness, pupil dilation, and quick breathing. These behaviors are not under the conscious control of the individual and are the body's responses to internal distress. For example, when some group members are anxious, they may clear their throat several times, or breath quickly, almost like snorting. When some group members get too close to threatening material they break out in a sweat, and others may lick their lips over and over. Fear may manifest itself when an individual becomes paler (blood draining from the face), while the rush of blood to the face (becoming red in the face) may signal anger or the immediacy of an attack. The body responds to the experiencing of the person without the person's conscious desire to do so.

Dilation of the pupils of the eye is usually associated with the degree of involvement or interest. Pupils are very dilated when interest or involvement is high and it is relatively easy to tell when interest or involvement has lessened if eye contact is maintained. The dilation of pupils is not an accurate source of information if the person has ingested medication or drugs that cause pupils to dilate. Most people who have not ingested medication or drugs will manifest constant changes in the degree of pupil dilation, and their nonverbal communication is an accurate barometer of what they are experiencing whereas the individual under the influence of alcohol or drugs will exhibit little or no variation in the extent of pupil dilation.

### Physical Characteristics/General Appearance

One's physical characteristics are a combination of heredity and personality factors. Characteristics such as height are a result of heredity, while characteristics such as fitness, weight, complexion, eye and hair color could be an outcome of the individual's personality and/or emotional state. For example, an individual may choose to change the eye color by wearing colored contacts, or change hair color with dye. Stress usually takes a physical toll as well as an emotional one, and observation of physical characteristics can also provide clues to the emotional state or functioning of the individual.

General appearance includes dress, hygiene, and grooming, all of which convey an impression of how the individual perceives him or herself, *or* wishes to be perceived by others. Cleanliness, tidiness, and appropriateness of dress give clues to the individual. For example, an individual who has poor personal hygiene and dirty clothes, and has made little or no effort to groom him/herself conveys that he/she cares little for self. It may be that the person is too depressed to make the effort, but the net effect is a lack of self-respect or self-caring. Another example is that females who are overly made up can appear to be hiding behind a mask. Makeup is being used to conceal rather than to enhance in this instance.

### Nonverbal Communication of Emotions

Darwin (1872) described inherited universal patterns of behavior for seven expressive emotions presented in Table 3.3: grief, joy, anger, fear, contempt, shame, and surprise. All of the patterns contain distinctive movements that can be used to promote understanding of these emotions, whether in oneself or in others. The group leader can have members "try on the emotions" or, if some members are experiencing that emotion, such as grief, have those members exaggerate the movements and body positions.

Tompkins (1963) identified eight emotions that are fundamental and appear to be inherited: interest and joy are positive; distress, fear, anger, contempt, and shame are negative; and surprise is "resetting." Positive emotions allow us to be excited by novelty and to enjoy the familiar, such as those we love. Negative emotions allow us to deal with life's crises and, as such, are adaptive mechanisms. The "resetting" emotion interrupts positive and negative ones to provide an opportunity for reorienting.

### Constructive Use of Nonverbal Behaviors

This discussion began with a charge to the group leader to become more aware of nonverbal behavior--both his or her own personal nonverbal behavior and that of clients. Becoming aware of one's own nonverbal behavior requires a great deal of self-knowledge and the willingness to allow oneself to become congruent in verbal and nonverbal communication. Realizing that your nonverbal behavior conveys an attitude, degree of acceptance, feelings and emotions, and level of interest is usually motivation enough to promote selfexploration. Learning the importance of and ways to "read" nonverbal behaviors of others enhances the group process. This may be especially important when using expressive processes in a group because these processes can bypass defenses and help the individual to access very important, sensitive, and often painful material. The group leader needs to be alert to these possibilities, which are usually manifested primarily through nonverbal communication, in order to help and guide the individual better in understanding and coping with the material. Remember, it is more important for the leader to understand the nonverbal communication than it is to make the individual aware of it. It is not necessary to point out the behavior, although there are times when it may be helpful.

**Table 3.3**
**Behaviors Associated with Emotions**

| Emotion | Body Positions/Movement |
|---|---|
| Grief--fresh and intense | Violent, frantic movements somewhat hyperactive |
| Grief--prolonged and intense | Lack of movement, depressed body position |
| Joy | Purposeless movements, such as, clapping hands, skipping, dancing, laughing |
| Anger | Erect body ready for action, mouth and teeth held tightly, fists clenched |
| Fear | Trembling, eyes open very wide, lack of motion |
| Contempt | Spitting, turning nose up |
| Shame | Body turned away, eyes turned down or away, body compression as if trying to hide |
| Surprise and Startle | Quick changes in body positions/movement, eyes and mouth open, eyebrows raised |

# 4

# THEORIES

## RATIONALE FOR WORKING WITH EXPRESSIVE PROCESSES

### Framework

Theories provide frameworks for understanding expressive processes: that is, creating, analyzing, and interpreting the material that emerges. It is assumed that the counselor will be knowledgeable about major counseling theories, and have in-depth knowledge of object relations, gestalt, existential, Jungian, and person-centered theories.

Why these theories and not some others? Almost any major counseling theory can incorporate use of expressive processes. These particular theories were selected because these are the ones that contributed most to my knowledge and development as a counselor educator. My students have responded favorably to these and have expressed an understanding of their usefulness. My recommendation is that the reader not feel bound to these theories, but use them as a starting point to understand how expressive processes can facilitate therapy.

### Object Relations Theories

Object Relations theories describe how individuals came to be as they are, the quality of their relationships with others, and focus on the psychological development of the individual from birth. Concepts incorporated by several object relations theorists explain what healthy development is and suggest ages at which stages as phases most likely occur, as well as variables that impact development. Many delays, interruptions, traumas, deficits, and other factors in development appear in symbolic form in products of expressive processes. The group leader is not expected to analyze or interpret the product; however, when group members explain their products, early developmental issues, particularly unresolved ones, are very likely to be present. The group leader will miss much valuable material if he/she is not familiar with psychological growth and development. The group members would continue to work on symptoms rather than underlying issue if the group leader is not knowledgable enough about psychological growth and development.

### Gestalt Theory

*Gestalt theory* contributes a here and now focus that is recommended when using expressive processes. The theory is also action-oriented, relies on the client to do the majority of the work, and strongly emphasizes feelings and emotions. This focus and emphasis are considered important when using expressive processes, for it is the individual who has the ability to understand him/herself, and to make changes. Feelings and emotions are also considered to be important as they contain most of the message as to how individuals perceive others, situations, events, and self. Learning to tune into feelings, express them appropriately, and understand them is a major part of therapeutic work.

### Existential Theory

*Existential theory* helps give an understanding of the individual's relationship to the universe. It broadens therapy to incorporate basic issues with which all humans struggle: responsibility, loneliness, indifference of the universe to individuals, importance of individuals to the universe, purpose in life, and inevitability of death and nonbeing. These very basic and complex issues appear in disguised ways but also impact the everyday functioning of individuals. Group leaders can be more effective if they can recognize when existential issues emerge and help members express and understand personal existential issues as well as the universality of these issues.

### Person-Centered Theory

*Person-centered theory* provides some basic concepts that define an appropriate therapeutic attitude for the group leader and suggests techniques for interaction with members. The concepts of empowering group members, being nonjudgmental, accepting and valuing members as worthwhile unique individuals, being nondirective in interactions, and using reflection and clarification are very useful in giving specific guidelines for making the most of expressive processes.

### Jungian Theory

*Jungian theory* is used because it emphasizes the power of the unconscious, and proposes that material from the unconscious appears in symbolic images. Many of the expressive processes described in the book assume that products are symbolic representations of unconscious material and symbols must be associated or analyzed for meanings. Jung also proposed a method for therapy whereby the individual gave personal meanings for symbols and images that emerged instead of therapists providing interpretations. He also devoted much time and effort to seeking to understand the messages conveyed by symbols as well as their universality.

## CONTRIBUTIONS OF SPECIFIC THEORIES

### Introduction

What follows is a brief summary and description of the components in each theory that has found to be of value when using expressive processes components such as major concepts, terms, understandings and applications to development. It is strongly recommended that the reader review these theories in more depth or, if unfamiliar with a particular theory, consult original sources for a deeper understanding.

## OBJECT RELATIONS

### Major Concepts

*Objects* in object relations theory refer to relations with others whether that relationship is internal, external, fantasized, or real. How and when these relationships develop or fail to develop determine the quality of relationships and functioning throughout one's life. Thus, it is important to understand the development of the psychological life for individuals if counseling is to be effective and the impact of early experiences or deprivation on present functioning and relationships.

It may be even more important to have an understanding of the framework that object relations theory provides when using creative or expressive processes in counseling. While the use proposed in this book does not involve interpretation of products by the group leader, he/she should understand how products may be reflective of relationships that stem from past experiences or interactions. Many products will illustrate the importance for the individual of psychological development concepts such as, transitional objects, incomplete separation, and/or individuation, projection, splitting, and representation. The group leader should be alert to possibilities and implications in the products that point to the impact of incomplete or delayed psychological development that continues to influence current functioning.

### Psychological Development

Object relations theorists assume that crucial psychological development begins with infancy. The quality of nurturing received, interaction with others, and fulfillment of needs are some of the variables that contribute to constructive and healthy psychological development. When any of these is missing, incomplete, or inadequate, the development of the individual is usually impaired. And, because it happens during infancy, memories are flawed and only the effect of events, affects, and impressions are left. Further, time distorts memory, leading to manifestations of behaviors and emotions that cannot be directly related or connected to past events. We really have no idea what infants can contain or hold, nor for how long, or what the impact can be. Major current object relational theorists and clinicians accept that conditions, such as borderline and narcissistic personality disorders, have their roots in the quality of nurturing received as an infant.

### Klein

Melanie Klein (1932) was one of the first to focus on object relations as a way of understanding psychological development. She specialized in therapy with children and drew much of her theory from clinical experiences and observations. Some of her basic concepts were projection, introjection, splitting, phantasy, and inner object. Therapy is focused on relieving anxieties around how inner realities control the way external realities are perceived, which, in turn, can lead to fears of destruction.

*Projection* is a concept that is used by other object relations theorists, and other theories, such as gestalt. *Projection* describes the process by which one puts onto another a part of one's self. This is not done consciously, and the projected part is usually a part of self that is considered to be undesirable. For example, I am angry but either cannot accept that I am angry, or repress angry feelings for one reason or the other. So that I do not have to own or feel my anger, I project it onto you and characterize you as angry. This projecting keeps me from having to experience the uncomfortable emotion and allows me to feel different or superior to you because I did not become angry, you did.

*Introjection* is the reverse of projection in that one takes into self a part of the other. Introjection is the process by which we become acculturated, understanding shoulds and oughts. We introject these from others without the introjection's necessarily being a conscious act. An example of introjection is when the child understands that something is disgusting by the look on the mother's or father's face. Whatever has been done may not, in and of itself, be disgusting, but because the feeling of others is of disgust (look on face), the child introjects it and becomes disgusted also. Many of the patterns of reaction and behavior can be traced to introjections from the early years.

*Splitting* refers to the inability to integrate or synthesize incompatible experiences or feelings, and because of the conflict they are kept separate, or split off. For example, it is difficult for the infant to accept that the mother can be both nurturing and frustrating. When the development of the ability to integrate these polarities is impaired, the two sides are kept separate and mother is either all good or all bad. This singularity in perception of others can be carried over into adulthood, and others are perceived and reacted to as totally positive or totally negative. Healthy development requires that one be able to see the polarities and resolve conflicting emotions, reactions, and so forth, by merging or synthesizing the polarities. Splitting off and denying or repressing either side results in negative impact on relationships.

*Phantasy*, in Kleinian terms, is the inner mental representation of instinctual drives, such as hunger. That is, the infant has certain instinctual drives that are experienced and/or controlled through mental imagery. The infant cannot, at this point, distinguish between reality and fantasy. This leads to the assumption and conviction that every discomfort or frustration is a personal, hostile attack (St. Clair 1986). Phantasy, in this context, is different from daydreams or fantasy. Fantasy is conceptualized as "not real" either in objective reality or in inner experiencing.

*Inner objects* is the term used by Klein to define inner representation of objects. The inner representation of an object is also a phantasy.

Klein was among the first to focus on the quality of nurturing received by the infant as crucial for healthy psychological development. Her emphasis was on the kind and extent of the relationship developed with the nurturer, usually the mother, from birth. How the infant perceived the relationship and constructed inner objects greatly influenced phantasies and their outcomes, for instance, the extent to which the infant felt discomfort and perceived it as a hostile attack from frustrating outside forces.

### Winnicott

Winnicott built on Klcin's theory by accepting the importance of early nurturing relationships but adding to it the importance of the surrounding environment. He proposed several concepts that are used extensively today: hallucination of omnipotence, good-enough-mother, true self and false self, and transitional object.

*Hallucination of omnipotence* refers to the infant's belief that he/she controls the external world and causes things to "be" or "happen." For example, the infant becomes hungry and, as if by magic, is fed. The inner fantasy is that the infant satisfies his or her own needs and brings the satisfying agent into existence. This can be seen in adult behavior when they get frustrated and angry or people that do not do or act in accord with their demands, needs, or wishes.

Another concept coined by Winnicott is the "*just good enough mother*." The meaning is that the parent, again it's usually the mother, provides that which is sufficient for the child's needs *at that stage of development*. In other words, the mother anticipates, adapts, and changes in constantly providing for the infant and child as he/she develops. When she does this, the infant begins to develop an awareness of the external world and to relate to it. Winnicott (1989) notes that meeting the minute to minute needs of the infant calls for a high level of healthy identification with the infant; however, it must not be liable to morbid preoccupation.

*True self--false self* is Winnicott's expression for that described by some others as the "observing ego." The assumption behind the concept is that good enough mothering allows the "real self" to feel safe enough to allow itself to gradually become aware of and come in contact with reality. When there is an absence of good enough mothering, the "false self" protects the "real self" from the perceived threatening aspects of reality and the external world is perceived and interacted with in a distorted way which builds false relationships and continues to be a mode of relating to others in later life. The "real self" allows individuals to be genuine and authentic in relationships.

*Transitional objects* are the first not-me thing or possession. Winnicott used the term to denote the infant's acceptance of a symbol. Transitional objects may be exemplified by the infant's thumb, blanket or toy.

**Mahler**

Margaret Mahler built on the object relation theories of Klein, Winnicott, and others. She, however, focused on describing the psychological birth and development of the individual. She described three developmental stages of psychological development; normal autism (birth to two months), normal symbiosis (two months to seven months), and separation-individuation.

*Normal autism* describes the infant's customary state after birth. Everything is perceived in terms of self. The infant cannot distinguish between self and not-self and, in that way, is autistic.

*Symbiosis* refers to "being one with the mother." The infant has begun to recognize that there is a need satisfying object in his or her world (usually the mother), but considers the object as one with self, that is, fused. Good enough mothering gradually introduces the infant to external reality by providing necessary and satisfying functions.

Separating and developing individuation are parallel developmental phases. *Separation* refers to psychological differentiation from the mother and incudes physical as well as psychological distancing, and disengagement. *Individuation* is an inner sense of independence from the symbiotic relationship. St. Clair (1986) writes that "borderline and narcissistic disorders seem to result from traumas and disturbance of developmental processes during the separation--individuation phase. Some of the symptoms of narcissism and borderline pathology that involve omnipotence, splitting, and grandiosity are behavioral manifestations of developmental tasks that were disturbed or not completed" (p. 117). The ability to conceptualize "me" and "not me" and tolerate the separation is a crucial developmental task. For some the task was never completed or was only partially completed leading to difficulties with relationships later or throughout life.

## GESTALT

### Major Concepts

*Gestalt theory* has a present-centered emphasis which does not discount the past or future but accepts that the present is significant and must be experienced in its fullest sense. Why the individual is or how he/she came to be as he/she is not as important as understanding what and who the person is. A gestalt therapist, in the purest form, does not have clients explore the past or project the future except as either can be experienced in the here and now. Some major concepts from gestalt therapy that are useful in expressive processes are the here and now, unfinished business, five layers of neurosis, introjection, projection, retroflection, and blocks to energy.

*The here and now* demands that awarenesses, energies, and experiencing be present centered. Feelings are not "talked about" but are experienced in the present. This is one way past events become a part of therapy. That is, feelings connected with past events are not described: they must be brought into the present and reexperienced. Relating stories or describing events allows feelings and emotions to become distanced or dissociated. If these are to be reintegrated or resolved, the intensity must be dealt with, and reexperiencing emotions allows this to happen. It is very difficult for clients to stay present-centered, and one way of avoiding intense affect is to "talking about," elaborately describing, and/or story telling. Expressive processes allow past experiences and associated feelings to be brought into the here and now and reexperienced in an environment that provides safety and support.

Becoming *present-centered* also allows awareness of unfinished business to emerge. Many of the expressive processes described in this book produce greater awareness of unfinished business. While this outcome may be most beneficial for the client, the counselor can also benefit by using expressive processes to become aware of his or her own unfinished business that may have countertransference implications.

*Unfinished business* refers to unintegrated or unresolved feelings or emotions connected to a prior event that continue to impact current experiencing or functioning. Unrecognized grief, resentments, anger, and other factors, continue to influence individuals sometimes, in unexpected ways. For example, an individual may continually seek approval from others in response to unfinished business, such as unresolved feelings around parental lack of approval. These individuals seek confirmation of their worthwhileness from others to an extent which prevents them from attaining true intimacy. Gestalt therapists emphasize becoming aware of unfinished business, and the means by which it continues to be avoided, and resolving affects connected to it.

### Working Through Layers to Psychological Maturity

Perls (1970) postulated five layers of neuroses: phony, phobic, impasse, implosive, and explosive. Each layer must be confronted and resolved in order for psychological maturity to occur. The *phony* layer is the superficial one where others are related to in terms of games, roles, stereotypes, and so on. Not being authentic prevents the real self from being known, and, hence, little or no intimacy can occur.

The *phobic layer* refers to what the psychoanalysts and others would term *resistance* or *defensive*. Denial and repression are used to prevent contact with parts of self that are considered undesirable. Individuals are fearful that if they recognized and accepted these aspects of self, then others could see these aspects and others would reject them.

Perls considered the *impasse layer* to be that where a sense of deadness and stuckness are experienced. There is, perhaps, an awareness of aspects of self that had been previously denied, but the individual could go no further. The individual does not feel capable of further movement on his or her own and does not trust or accept his or her own inner resources. In order not to feel "dead" some individuals seek the support of the environment and attempt to manipulate it. Perls felt the impasse layer "deadness" had to be experienced, not avoided, before reaching the implosive layer when asked about feelings. Those at this layer are prone to answer, "Nothing," or "I feel numb," or "I do not know."

The *implosive layer* contains the unpleasant feelings and emotions that have been avoided by overlaying them with the other three layers. These feelings and emotions must be fully experienced and integrated before the explosive layer can be reached.

The *explosive layer* is termed this because individuals who reach this layer report on a "bursting through" experience. The bursting through may be a freeing from a burden or a freeing up of creative energy. It is there that there is a release of energy, energy that has been used to avoid knowing and accepting self fully. By letting go of roles, preconceptions about others, games, and so on, the individual can be authentic and attain true intimacy.

### Resistance

In gestalt theory there are three forms of *resistance*: introjection, projection, and retroflection. *Introjection* refers to the passive and uncritical acceptance and incorporation of the beliefs, standards, and attitudes of others. Introjects come from the environment and, if not critically examined and then freely adopted or rejected, cause the individual to act in accord with the needs, desires, and dictates of others rather than acting on personal needs and desires. Introjects can prevent and individual from knowing and accepting self.

*Projections* allow individuals to avoid taking responsibility for themselves and their feelings. It refers to disowning parts of self and putting them onto others. Projecting allows denial to persist and distortions of others to occur, thereby having a negative impact on relationships. For example, if I am angry, but do not accept or own my anger, I will project it on to someone else and term them as angry, and react to them as if they are angry. If the other person is not angry, he/she will become confused at my reaction.

When one turns back on self what he/she would like to do to others, it is termed *retroflection*. People who engage in self-destructive behaviors are demonstrating retroflection. They are usually fearful of the consequences of lashing out at others and, so, they injure themselves instead.

## EXISTENTIALISM

### Major Focus

*Existential* perspectives provide a basis for using expressive techniques because the philosophy assumes that being human implies a continuing exploration of who we are and the world around us. Being, as such, is not static and humans constantly recreate themselves. Further, the *existential* perspective asserts that humans have the capacity for self-awareness, for freedom and responsibility, for discovery of self-identify and establishment of meaningful relationships, attempts to discover or establish purpose in and of life, acceptance of anxiety as a given in life, and awareness of one's own death. Many of these existential issues continually emerge in therapy and in products of expressive processes. Recognizing their existence can add another dimension to growth and psychological maturity.

### Self-Awareness

Accepting that everyone has the capacity for self-awareness opens up vistas for personal growth and development. Becoming aware of choices, decisions, and potentials enriches and expands the capacity for living. Becoming aware is one of the basic needs for individuals in search of psychological maturity. Further, counselors and other therapists who accept the client's capacity for self-awareness realize that the seed potentials for growth and development lie within the individual and not in techniques or expertise.

### Freedom and Responsibility

Freedom and responsibility imply that individuals create their lives, through either the choices and decisions they make or, do not make. While many environmental and life circumstances may not be under the individual's control, continuing to blame others is counterproductive for him or her. Even under the most horrendous conditions, humans can assume responsibility and make conscious choices. Viktor Frankl graphically illustrates this in his account of how people behaved in concentration camps. Under the most vile and dehumanizing conditions imaginable, some were able to maintain their humanity. His book *Man's Search for Meaning* should be required reading for all therapists.

If an individual is to find self-identity, then he/she must have the courage to explore, create, and discover his or her core being. This search involves not merely accepting standards, expectations, values, attitudes, and so on, of others, but also establishing personal ones that are freely chosen. Expressive processes provide an opportunity to examine one's self and explore choices.

### Loneliness

Along with exploration of self, the individual has to allow him or herself to experience loneliness, meaninglessness, despair, and anxiety. Most people spend enormous time and energy avoiding feeling these emotions. They block off these very uncomfortable emotions, fill up time with activities, and use other means to avoid experiencing them. These emotions put us in touch with the finiteness of life, the aloneness or insulation of each of us, and allow the emergence of the capacity to relate in meaningful ways to others. Only when one is comfortable with oneself can one then have the capacity to be truly intimate with others. Many products of expressive processes illustrate the fear or incapacity to attain or maintain intimacy with others.

### Creating Meaning

Challenging, struggling to understand, and creating meaning for life underlie much human endeavor. Many have difficulty in establishing a life's direction because they have not examined and determined, for themselves, the meaning of their lives. Existential theory maintains that all of us must establish our own meaning and purpose. However, many individuals continue to live their lives according to the unquestioned standards and dictates of others. They do not examine them critically and make a conscious choice to accept them, thereby giving meaning to their lives and accepting responsibility. I have always liked the saying that the meaning life has is that which you give it.

### Anxiety

*Anxiety* is defined both as "feeling of uncertainty or uneasiness about the future," and as "eager desire tinged with fear" (*Webster's Dictionary* 1983). Corey (1991) proposes that existential anxiety is experienced when one moves out to the unknown after choosing to do so and accepting responsibility. May (1981) links freedom and anxiety by noting that exercising one's freedom promotes existential anxiety.

Existential anxiety, if confronted, can be a source of creativity and growth. While it is a frightening and uncomfortable experience, the benefits can be enormous and satisfying. Confronting anxiety expands awareness of choices and potentials, while seeking to alleviate anxiety, or repressing or denying it, leads to more constriction and much less awareness and more frustration.

### Death

Feifel (1963) concluded that while birth is an uncontrollable event, the manner of departure (death) reflects one's philosophy of life and death. He goes on to point out, "Life is not comprehended truly or lived fully unless the idea of death is grappled with honestly."

Death is inevitable, and facing the fact that one will cease to exist is very difficult and frightening. Many existential theorists and therapists view anxiety about death as a human condition that influences other aspects of life. Yalom (1985) points out in his review of research on the presence of existential factors in group therapy that these factors appear to always be present even if they are not recognized or openly addressed. Death, as an existential factor, is one of the most important factors, and the extent to which the individual has considered it plays a significant role in the level, intensity, and meaning he or she has in life.

## PERSON-CENTERED

### Major Concepts

*Person-centered theory* includes several concepts that are applicable to use of expressive processes as described in this book. Most importantly, the concepts refer to the attitudes, expertise, and "personhood" of the counselor. Those who can become adept in using the concepts *and* internalize them so that they are a part of their belief system will experience greater therapeutic effectiveness when using expressive processes. The primary concepts referred to are empowering the client, maintaining a nonjudgmental attitude, making a nondirective exploration of meanings from the products, having an acceptance of and positive regard for clients, and using reflection and clarification when processing. These characteristics are particularly useful in group where group members also assume some responsibility for their therapy.

### Empowering the Client

Carl Rogers (1951) pioneered person-centered theory and therapy. He was one of the first to place or give responsibility to the client for the course of his or her therapy. Empowering clients to take charge and assume responsibility prevents them from being in a victim, patient, or other dependent role where the counselor is the expert and has the answers. The person-centered approach assumes that the answers lie within the individual.

### Being Nonjudgmental

If one accepts that answers lie within the client, then the counselor also has to be nonjudgmental about what emerges. It is not always easy to be nonevaluative, and a counselor who has not become aware of and worked through major countertransference issues will unwittingly engender much resistance by evaluating and judging in some way. All of the directions given in this book caution the group leader to take care not to make evaluative or judgmental comments, even positive ones. Most find it relatively easy not to make negative judgmental or evaluative comments, but find it much harder not to make positive ones. This is especially important when working with groups. A compliment or positive statement about a product to one member can easily be misunderstood by others as saying that their product is not as appreciated by the leader. Further, you may not know the member at the deepest level to be confident as to what his or her feelings are about the product, perceptions of the event or situation that led to the product, transferences, or other unconscious material, so that a positive statement may not be appropriate at this time. A group leader needs to develop a range of neutral and encouraging comments because saying nothing may be perceived as disapproval by some members.

### Acceptance

Group members who feel that the leader accepts them as worthwhile, unique individuals are more apt to feel that they are safe and cared for. Individuals who have their safety needs met are more likely to enter into a therapeutic relationship with the leader, feel understood, lower defenses, and be more willing to engage in exploration of their resistances. In short, members become willing participants and therapy flourishes. I am not sure that an accepting attitude can be faked for very long. There are those who can mask their true feelings about others, but it is very difficult to sustain fakery at a level that prevents the others from knowing. They may not verbalize their perceptions that your responses are not sincere, but little of therapeutic consequence takes place, and defenses and resistances remain firmly entrenched. The group leader who is genuine, showing caring and respect for group members is conveying acceptance.

### Nondirective Interventions

Person-centered theory uses what is termed *nondirective group leader interventions*. This proposes that group members lead the way, and through use of certain interactional skills, such as empathic listening and responding, the leader guides members in self-exploration. In other words, the group leader does not decide what is important for members to focus on and insist that they explore it, and if they do not, then term it resistance. Having a nondirective emphasis when processing expressive processes allows group members to feel safe, accepted, valued, and thereby, lowering of defenses is more likely, thus allowing relevant material to emerge in a form that can be accepted and used by them. This does not mean that the leader says nothing or does not guide members. Nothing could be further from the truth. The leader can pose open-ended questions and statements that help the client reflect on the experience and make statements that highlight the process. See Chapter 5 for specific guidelines. It must be emphasized that being nondirective does not mean doing or saying nothing. The group leader who does or says little or nothing can provoke great anxiety which does not promote feelings of safety and trust.

### Techniques

Techniques of person-centered therapy that are particularly useful are reflection and clarification. When a group member has his or her feelings, emotions, and thoughts reflected, much becomes clearer. For example, confusion and/or conflict around an issue may not be apparent or may even be denied. Reflecting what was expressed; not elaborating, questioning, or interpreting, can help the person accept his or her feelings, emotions, or thoughts. The member produced them; the group leader did not. Clarification performs the same functions in another way. Asking for clarification on certain points, clearing up conflicting statements, and/or pointing out confusion aids in self-understanding. Reflecting is also useful when making group-as-a-whole interventions. Restating or paraphrasing what various group members said and tying it together can help the group understand what the group is revealing or working on.

## ANALYTICAL PSYCHOLOGY

### Major Concepts

*Analytical or Jungian psychology* has many concepts uniquely suitable in using expressive processes. Jung felt that the unconscious was very important and devoted considerable effort to gaining understanding of it and how material from the unconscious manifests itself in symbolic form. He proposed that there was both an individual component to the unconscious and an inherited component, which he termed *the collective unconscious*. Because of his emphasis on accessing and understanding the unconscious, symbols, myths, religion, and rituals were explored in depth.

The personal unconscious was felt to be a container of material that was once conscious but is now repressed and denied. Personal events, situations, people, and so on, make up the material in the personal unconscious. While this material may not be readily available to the individual, it can be allowed to emerge, worked with, and then left in the conscious or returned to the unconscious.

The *collective unconscious* was defined as the reservoir of all of the experiences of humans throughout the ages which is passed on and repeated in each one of us. Jung (1958) found that similar symbols and themes appeared in diverse cultures throughout the world, and that these same symbols and themes appeared in his patients' dreams and fantasies.

### Concepts for Understanding Process and Products

Some primary concepts that have been useful in understanding the process and products of expressive processes are archetypes, shadow, and non-interpretative methods. All of these concepts assume the importance of the unconscious and how its material can be accessed and understood.

*Archetypes* are the images of universal experiences throughout the ages that reside in the collective unconscious, continuing to influence the psyche and, on an unconscious level, the behavior of individuals. The major archetypes that are manifested in dreams and fantasies are magic, the hero, the child, God, death, power, and the wise old man. These archetypes appear in almost every culture from the beginning of recorded human history and continue to appear in dreams today. Some guided imagery exercises are designed around these universal archetypes.

Other archetypes that were explored by Jung were the persona, animus, anima, and shadow. The *persona* is the mask that is used for public roles: that is, how one presents him or herself to others. Because we have to play a variety of roles, a mask that hides the real self is used to succeed in getting along with a wide diversity of people with whom we interact. The danger in using a persona is that one may then come to believe that that is the real "self" and fail to develop other aspects of personality. Campbell (1973) extended the concept to suggest that each person has a series of masks and that simply taking one off did not provide access to the "real self." The real self may be difficult to uncover as it is hidden beneath a series of masks.

The *animus and anima archetypes* are the names given to the collection of male and female psychological characteristics present in each of us. The archetype for males is the *anima:* the collection of female characteristics that reside in his unconscious and impact his psychological self in indirect ways. For the female, the archetype is the *animus,* which is the collection of male characteristics residing in her unconscious and impacting her psychological self. When individuals seek to deny any part of their selves, either consciously or unconsciously, conflict results. Jung felt that all humans had male or female external characteristics, and all have the internal psychological characteristics of male and female. Being fully human means being able to express both sides.

The *shadow archetype* is considered to be the unacceptable and unacknowledged side of self that usually contains the basic, primitive, animal instincts. The shadow also contains the energies that promote vitality, creativity and spontaneity. When one seeks to suppress unacceptable parts of self, the result is a lowering of vitality, creativity, and spontaneity. The task is to suppress the primitive impulses that are destructive to self and others, but allow those desirable aspects of self to emerge.

### Techniques

Jung introduced *noninterpretative methods,* recommending that instead of the therapist's interpreting for the patient, the individual supply meanings for his or her images. He felt that interpreting interrupted the process of allowing unconscious processes to become conscious. Experiencing *fantasies*, that is, the symbolic means of making unconscious processes conscious, was of more importance than making an intellectual interpretation. Understanding the message of the symbols relies on their personal meanings for the individual.

Two techniques developed were amplification and subjective amplification. *Amplification* is a rational expansion of an image or symbol. Describing the image and making statements about what it signifies to you help to clarify meanings. For example, an image of a hat could be expanded to describe it as decorative, worn to church, covering hair, concealing beauty. All of the descriptions could be woven together to produce a meaning that incorporates associations such as a time when hats were required, special occasions, and a period when attractions were hidden.

In *subjective amplification* the person supplies his or her own unique associations. The counselor and others do not suggest or imply meanings, only the individual does so. There are several advantages to this approach, not the least of which is that the individual is more likely to accept a meaning or association that he/she supplies.

# 5

# GUIDELINES

## ETHICAL CONSIDERATIONS

### Major Issues

Primary ethical considerations when using expressive processes are confidentiality, degree of psychological risk to group members, involuntary membership, and preparation of the leader. It is imperative that the leader be familiar with legal and ethical requirements of his or her professional organization, the agency or organization with whom he/she works, and the local, state, and federal governments regulations and/or laws.

### Confidentiality

While confidentiality is encouraged in groups and is a part of expected behavior, it must be reemphasized when using expressive processes as unexpected personal material may emerge and be disclosed. These processes can facilitate access to repressed and/or denied events, primitive feelings and emotions, and situations considered by the individual to be shameful. Although group members are in control of the amount and extent of self-disclosure, the intensity of affect aroused may encourage them to reveal a great deal, some of which is very sensitive. Trust and safety may have developed within the group to the extent where members feel comfortable with disclosing the material that emerges during the exercise in the group, and confidentiality is a crucial component in maintaining trust and feeling safe.

### Psychological Risk

The group leader should assess the degree of psychological maturity of each member and not use activities or processes that put members at risk. Many expressive processes evoke sensitive material and intense emotions that may be difficult for some members to handle. The leader should take care not only to select appropriate activities, but to also monitor members throughout the session and focus processing of activities appropriately. *Focusing processing* means keeping the analyses at a level the individual members can handle, and not putting them in a situation where they become overwhelmed with anxiety and/or other intense affect. This does not mean that the leader should guard against doing anything that would bring about crying. Tears can be beneficial and healing and, thus, are an appropriate response. Group leaders should assess the potential psychological risks of an activity before initiating it.

### Informed Consent

*Informed consent* usually refers to becoming a group member. However, part of knowing what is to be expected in the group would be having a knowledge of any expressive processes used. These may not have been preselected, but members should be informed about the particular expressive technique *prior to its use*. The purpose of using the activity, a brief description, and expected outcomes are considered to be minimum requirements. The leader may also wish to give permission for nonparticipation or ask for members' agreement to use the procedure. At any rate, members should have some idea of what they may experience as a result of the activity and what the leader will do to insure safety.

### Involuntary Membership

Involuntary membership carries its own barriers. When group membership is mandated, increased resistance, continuing concern over invasion of privacy and maintenance of confidentiality, and skepticism about the efficacy of the group occur. Expressive processes are effective ways around some of these barriers as well as the individual ones. For that reason, caution must be exercised. These group members may have very valid reasons for maintaining their resistance and denial because of their situation, such as fears of reprisal. They may not be living in a psychologically safe situation and may realistically fear inappropriate use of personal material by other group members or, if confidentiality is breached, by someone outside the group. Activities and processes that emphasize personal and private learning, such as guided writing, may be useful. The leader can also structure processing so that expressing affect is emphasized and personal material need not be shared.

### Professional Preparation

Leaders who use expressive techniques should have professional preparation in counseling and psychological theories, techniques, group leadership and experience as a participant with any technique used as well as instruction in use of the technique, activity, or process. The ability to use what emerges from the activity or process effectively is much more important than the capacity to structure it. Helping group members to become aware, clarify, analyze, and integrate emergent material is therapeutic. The skill and preparation of the leader are crucial to effective use of expressive techniques.

## PROCEDURES FOR USING EXPRESSIVE PROCESSES

There are certain procedures to be attended to in order to facilitate the use of any expressive process in the group. The primary ones are planning, setting goals and objectives for the exercise and the expected outcome or impact on the group, estimating the psychological readiness of members, and selecting appropriate exercises.

### Planning

It is preferable that expressive processes be planned. Planning allows adequate consideration of major concerns that contribute to successful use, concerns such as objective(s), psychological maturity and readiness of group members, and selection of the most appropriate activity. There are some processes that can be used spontaneously, such as role play and guided imagery, but even these are more effective if planned.

### Goals, Objectives

The leader should have a clear goal or objective in mind when using an expressive process. For example, using one could help resolve a group impasse; facilitate uncovering blocked awareness of issues for members or the group; relieve tension that is counterproductive to the therapeutic process; access repressed, suppressed, or denied material; clarify feelings and emotions; and highlight issues/problems/concerns. The leader should be able to articulate a goal or objective clearly for the group. Members will want to know why such an activity is proposed, and what benefit(s) they can expect. There are occasions where the process will have an effect other than or in addition to that which was planned. The leader needs to be flexible and knowledgeable enough to handle most unexpected events or situations so that they are constructive rather than disruptive or destructive. Chapters 7 through 12 on the different expressive processes give suggested uses or objectives, and many more uses are possible.

### Readiness of Members

Major concerns for the leader are the psychological readiness and maturity of group members. Any expressive process initiated should be viewed as facilitative, and selected with that objective in mind. You don't want to present group members with more than they can handle. Indeed, it may be useful to present them with less so that they are eager to do more. One question the leader can consider is "How much intense affect can members safely handle?" The idea is to introduce just enough tension so that new avenues can be explored, but not so much that individuals shut down. Members should not be so comfortable that all they get from the experience is a "feel good" response. New awarenesses and learnings should also be expected.

### Selection of Appropriate Exercise

After reading Chapters 7-12 on the expressive processes, group leaders should have a better understanding of the possibilities and limitations of each. This understanding, together with their own degree of comfort with each process and knowledge of group members psychological readiness and maturity, should provide a basis for selecting appropriate expressive processes. Experience will be the most helpful in knowing which exercise would be most beneficial for the group and its members at a particular time in the group's life. However, some guidance is provided in Chapters 7-12 and in Chapter 6.

### Member Variables

Group members may be unfamiliar with some of the processes or may not feel comfortable with their ability to produce acceptable products. For example, most people are uncomfortable when faced with a drawing or sculpting activity. They may have the perception that artistic ability or talent is called for but feel that they have little or none. Encouragement to try the activity along with an accepting, nonjudgmental attitude of the group leader helps promote confidence and a willingness to participate. It would be unusual for group members to resist to the point where the activity has to be scrapped; however, the leader should be alert to the possibility that resistance may be so intense that insisting on doing the activity would be counterproductive. In this instance, the leader should be willing to make the necessary adjustments. Such resistance is significant and the opportunity to explore it should be seized. Exploring this degree of resistance would be more important than proceeding with the proposed activity.

### Time Available

Another major concern when selecting an expressive process is the time available in a session to complete the activity, plus adequate time for processing. The group leader should ensure that adequate time is available for objectives and directions to be given, the activity to be completed, and, most importantly, the experience to be adequately processed. Enough time should be available for each member to share some part of the experience and to explore meanings and/or awarenesses. If there is not enough time, some members may be left dangling or feel cut off. The moment of awareness, learning, or understanding may be lost, and considerable time may be needed before it can be recaptured. If the expressive process has produced very intense affect, the leader may wish to extend the session so that it can be adequately processed, be available for consultation *on this experience* for members outside the group, or devise some method for helping members to handle the affect. It is a good practice to begin the next session with a checkup and/or unfinished business around the intense affect aroused.

## PREPARATION TASKS FOR THE LEADER

### Decisions and Choices

Planning facilitates use of expressive processes. Tasks such as gathering materials and deciding on a method for responding are organizational aspects that allow the leader to focus more on process and attend to members when sensitive material emerges. The leader should not have to concern him or herself with anything other than the exercise and reactions of group members. All else should be taken care of in advance.

### Materials

All materials for the activity should be gathered before the group session begins. Valuable time is lost if they have to be located once it begins. The leader has the responsibility to secure adequate materials to conduct the experience efficiently. Most materials needed are simple and easily found or purchased.

I have found it useful to keep a minimum of supplies on hand: such as newsprint, sets of felt tip pens, masking tape, index cards, and oil pastels. I also routinely save catalogues and magazines for collages so that when an opportunity arises I am not searching for these materials.

If music is going to be used, then appropriate tapes or compact disks should be on hand as well as the necessary playing equipment. In choosing equipment, try to select ones that do not make a loud noise when turned on or off. A loud click can be very distracting to participants.

### Response Modes

Choose the method by which group members will make a response, such as drawing, writing, talking. In order to allow all members to make a response, remember that drawing takes less time than writing, and writing takes less time than talking about the experience. When members take turns recounting their experiences, there is a tendency to elaborate or explore and/or for other members or the leader to ask questions, all of which increase the time one member takes to tell about his or her experiences. Sensitive material emerges and it is the rare leader who can pass up the opportunity to deepen the experience for that member. However, by exploring in more depth with that member, other members are left dangling. Whatever is done should provide for all members to have an opportunity to present or share their personal experience with the activity.

Drawing is a mode of response that takes the least amount of time and produces a product that has significance. Even though it is not interpreted, or used as an art therapist would use it, a drawing has more relevant personal associations for the group member. Drawings can also allow the group member to reflect on the experience and decide what part to disclose to the group at this time. It is interesting to me that most group members tend to want to tell more when they use a drawing than either through writing or talking about their experience. For some reason they seem to feel less threatened when there is the possibility that they can show their drawing and make personal associations than when they write or tell about the experience.

Writing, for some members, is easier than drawing. When group members are very educated and comfortable with words, they tend to want to write in preference to drawing. However, drawing the response is more likely to bypass defenses, since members cannot hide behind words or retreat into the cognitive state and are more likely to remain connected with affects aroused by the experience. This is one reason that highly verbal people prefer to use words and the reason that I like to use drawing as a response mode. Writing also takes longer to finish than does drawing and when members begin to share the experience they remain more detached.

### Structuring the Exercise

The leader can begin by telling members that he/she would like to use the expressive technique chosen, such as a guided imagery, the objective for the exercise, and give a description of the activity. It is not necessary to present all the objectives at this time, if by doing so the outcome would be compromised. However, members should know that there is a reason for participating and some expected benefits for them as individuals or for the group.

It is at this point that the leader should tune in to the degree of reluctance and resistance to determine whether it is wise to continue. Resistance or reluctance may not be expressed directly and openly but may be disguised as repetitive questions. If there is resistance from several members consider dropping the exercise and explore the feelings around the proposed exercise. If only one member is resistant give that member permission not to participate. It may also be helpful to explore with the other members feelings around the nonparticipation in a *non-judgmental* way. The intent is not to bring group pressure on the non-participating member but to determine if that member is containing all of the resistance for the group. Assuming that members are willing to try the activity, the leader can then distribute materials before giving directions. It is best that materials be distributed before beginning the activity. Members can then write or draw immediately after the experience and stay more in touch with the material and affects generated.

Directions should be given for completion of the activity. Specific directions for each expressive process will be found in the relevant chapter. After giving directions, time should be allowed for questions and clarification. When first using an activity, the leader may find it useful to write out all directions so as not to forget to mention something important to completion of the activity.

General and specific procedures for each expressive process are presented in the chapter that describes a specific expressive process, such as the chapter on dreams.

## LEADER TASKS DURING THE EXERCISE

### Observations

The leader must carefully observe members during the experience. Observation of the effect of the activity, possible resistances, when sensitive material is touched on, and/or intensity of affect provides useful clues for processing and future exploration. Much of what is observed is nonverbal behavior. Verbalizations are useful, but nonverbal behavior reveals the greater part of what may be going on for and with the member(s).

Observation of *postural cues* provides some evidence of the degree of tension and anxiety being experienced. Tension is indicated by the degree or tightness of muscles and lack of movement. Anxiety is conveyed when there is considerable movement of one part of the body, such as a jiggling foot, eyes that cannot seem to focus on one thing but shift quickly. A depressed posture of slumping or otherwise pulling into self may be observed and noted. It is particularly useful to observe these cues while members are drawing or writing.

Other nonverbal behaviors while drawing, writing or telling about an experience that are useful to observe are clusters of gestures used and degree of involvement cues such as quickness of response, thoughtfulness, facial expression, and playfulness. These observations are used to help the leader know when to attend to a particular member.

*Gestures* are best examined in clusters. While research may have attached some meanings to individual gestures, such as hand to face indicting thoughtfulness or evaluation, these are not necessarily universal nor may they be meaningful for the specific group member at that particular time. However, if clusters are used judiciously, then meanings may be more accurate. For example, wringing of hands together with tears or a facial indication of distress can usually be interpreted more accurately than either alone.

### Responding

The *quickness with which members respond*, that is, drawing or writing, may indicate the level of resistance or degree of awareness. A quick response may indicate that the member is eager to record what was experienced, the new learnings or awarenesses. Or it may indicate that he/she hasn't allowed him or herself to participate in the activity at a significant level and has remained superficial. The product usually reveals which interpretation is correct. For example, I have had students who wanted to participate in an experience but did not want to get in touch with relevant material so they would quickly draw or write after the activity. Although much more was revealed than they were aware of or had intended, the product was easily seen as much more superficial than the one by someone who allowed him or herself to participate deeply in the activity.

Members who take considerable time to respond may be analyzing, evaluating, and judging what emerged for them and may be resisting accepting the material as they experienced it. They are taking their time to come up with a response that they can find acceptable. This, of course, is resistance. They may be resisting the awarenesses that emerged or may be monitoring their response so that the leader and other members will not be knowledgeable about the material. Shame, guilt, and so on, may play a part in the resistance. It really doesn't matter at this point the reason for the resistance, and the leader is better off noting it for him or herself and *not addressing it openly at this time.* Pointing out resistances has a compounding effect on other members in the group and can make them fearful that their resistances will also be perceived and brought out. This makes them even more cautious in disclosing about their experience and lessens the effectiveness of the expressive process.

### The Product

Observe the *degree of consideration given* to the product. Some members go to great lengths to make sure their product reflects as much of their experience as possible, while others appear to give it almost no thought. Those who reflect on the experience and try to glean as much meaning as possible get more out of the activity than those who do not. However, some who appear not to reflect may have gotten in touch with some sensitive or threatening material and their product is pared down to essentials. Close observation of affect usually indicates whether the response is a superficial one or reflects essential sensitive material. In the latter case, the leader would want to make sure that the member was taken care of before leaving the session.

### Facial Expressions

*Facial expressions* are usually good indicators of feelings and emotions even when the individual may be consciously trying to suppress them or lessen their intensity. Group leaders will find it useful to pay close attention to facial expressions during the activity, making of a product, and processing. Even when members try to deny what they are feeling, their facial expressions reflect their true experiencing. Pay close attention to the eyes and their movement. Intense involvement is usually indicated when the pupils enlarge. Sensitive material or intense affect may be indicated by lack of eye contact when there has been fairly consistent eye contact previously. Eyes that roam and do not seem to be able to focus on anyone or anything for very long may signal internal anxiety. It is at this point that leaders will want to check in with the member and give him or her an opportunity to express, explore, and handle the affect around the emergent material. Further exploration can be left to future sessions, but *the affect should be dealt with immediately.*

### Outcomes

If an expressive process is used as a tension reliever the leader will want to observe whether members become playful. After all, the objective was to lighten up a little and it is helpful to know whether that objective has been attained. Pay particular attention to any member who seems to remain mired in tension or anxiety. He/she may be experiencing overwhelming pressure that needs the leader's intervention. The person may be unable to let go and need additional attention to his or her plight. The ability to laugh and play is an indicator of emotional and mental wellness, and the degree of playfulness during an expressive process designed to produce it tells the leader a great deal about group members.

One nonverbal gesture that seems to be significant in indicating whether an individual is participating or responding on an emotional level or, on a cognitive level, is the position of the palms. Palms up usually indicate a primary cognitive level and palms down, an emotional one. Note shifts of palms while talking and check out whether the person is emotionally involved or is "talking about" the situation or experience. It may be best if the leader does not reveal what nonverbal gesture led to the question or statement as it has been my experience that group members are careful to monitor their hand movements and this clue can no longer be used effectively.

The group leader is very busy and involved during an expressive process even though he/she may not appear to be doing anything. I find it useful to make notes to myself during the activity as a focus for personalizing processing after the exercise or activity. It is then possible to highlight specific behaviors for individuals during processing of the exercise.

## PROCESSING THE EXPERIENCE

### Outcomes of Processing

Processing is the stage or phase where most of the therapeutic work is done and safety issues addressed. Careful processing by the leader promotes awarenesses, understanding, acceptance, and willingness to go deeper. It is essential for the leader to be alert, aware, and sensitive and to demonstrate expertise. Following are some suggested focuses, emphases and guidelines However, the attitude of the leader will be most important. The most facilitative attitude is one that is nonjudgmental, caring, accepting, and conveys confidence in group members to confront and work through material that emerged during the activity. It is also important not to infer motives but to report on observed behavior.

### Themes and Issues

While members are sharing their products and/or experiences, note the themes and issues among and between individuals. This data can be used in linking and highlighting universality that is not readily apparent to members. Oft times, commonalities are overlooked because situations and events are individualistic, and when group members are caught up in their own experiencing, are not recognized.

Themes and issues for individual group members may also reflect themes and issues for the group. When many, or most, group members have the same theme or issue, it is likely also to be one for the group and is probably affecting the group in some way. Depending on the leader's theoretical orientation, he/she will decide whether to make individual or group interventions.

### Associations

During processing the leader should begin to make associations between what emerged from the activity, present or current experiencing for individuals and the group, and continuing issues related to significant past events. Characteristic ways of handling affect and response should also be noted. It is not always necessary to discuss these associations at this point, they can be brought up at the next session. It is much more important to have reporting or input from each member than it is to highlight these associations. By all means, do highlight them if there is time to do so and highlighting would result in deepening the experience for either individuals, the group, or both.

### Feelings and Emotions

It is crucial that there be a major emphasis on feelings and emotions aroused and experienced throughout the activity: creating, reporting, and processing. Members should be encouraged to identify, label, and verbalize these feelings and emotions even if they do not relate the associations, connections, situations, events, or people they identify as a part of these affects. In other words, at this time they do not have to tell why they have these feelings and emotions; however, it is hoped that they will continue to explore their personal experiencing. The leader should note these for possible future interventions.

As members talk about their experiencing and products, the leader can point out what is missing (if anything) if the missing component is significant. For example, if a group member has disclosed a significant family event or situation and the same event or situation was brought up for him or her during the activity but the person left out a primary person in their reporting, the leader could point out the omission and allow the person to draw implications. Another instance where an omission could be pointed out is if logically one would expect to see something and it's absent. An example would be if the event or situation were taking place outside in the summertime and trees in the drawing had no leaves.

Processing should always involve asking members to report on feelings after the activity, recording, and sharing are over. This provides an opportunity to summarize feelings and emotions around the experience. Ask for comments about the usefulness of the activity, what was easy, what was hard, what they liked, and what they did not like. This kind of feedback allows the leader to evaluate an activity more fully. Do be careful not to discard an activity because group members did not like it or felt that they did not get much from doing it that would assist them therapeutically. It may not have worked for this group but may work for another group. Sometimes, the benefits are not immediately apparent to group members but are recognized later. An example of this was when a fairy tale expressive process was used with an eating disorder group. One member did not feel the activity was beneficial for her. However, she referred to what emerged for her personally four sessions later and continued to make comments about it in future sessions.

### Summarize

The leader should always summarize at the end of the group. Describe some of what was observed as members participated; identify intense emotions aroused, group issues/themes, and, if appropriate, individual issues/themes. Suggest that member continue to reflect on what emerged for them from the experience and to explore significant material. Future sessions could be built around the new or rediscovered awarenesses, knowledge, and understandings.

# 6

# APPLICATIONS

## RATIONALE

### Primary Outcomes for Expressive Processes

Using expressive processes in groups increases the intensity of the experience, promotes individual participation, helps clarify individual and group themes and issues, highlights commonality among group members, promotes awareness of the impact of members behavior on group functioning, and can be used to confront directly hidden agendas or problems that are impeding group process. Expressive processes are most beneficial when used to accomplish a specific goal and have been carefully selected with the needs of members and of the group taken into consideration: the stage of the group, maturity and level of self-awareness of members, nature of the problem being addressed, and willingness of members to risk new or unfamiliar activities. There are many benefits to be gained from using expressive processes in group for both the individual and the group.

## ADVANTAGES OF EXPRESSIVE PROCESSES

### Self-generated

There are many advantages to judicial use of expressive techniques with groups. One advantage is that that which is produced is generated from the individual and is not the result of outside influence, except for structuring the task. Another advantage is that every member in the group can participate and work on his or her issue(s) at the same time. When one person is verbalizing his or her issues, he/she receives all the attention and it is difficult to learn to work on personal issues while someone else is working on his or hers orally. Another primary advantage for self-generated products is the increased willingness of the group members to accept what emerged and to explore it to extract as much information as possible. Resistance to the material is reduced. There are others advantages which will be discussed later in the chapter.

### Increases Intensity

There is something about the group setting that intensifies the reactions and responses to expressive processes. Members appear to work harder, be more willing to explore personal issues in depth, accept deeper associations, and lower defenses to access relevant material. Providing an opportunity to share with other members of the group appears to contribute to intensification of the experience and lessen denial. I do not know why but the same expressive process used with an individual does not produce the same level of intensity as when it is used with a group.

### Promotes Self-exploration

There may be some reluctance at first when members are first asked to participate in these processes. Many adults and many children are fearful that their products will not be satisfactory or "right" and so will resist. With encouragement and a nonjudgmental attitude of the group leader, members will attempt them, enjoy them, and learn from them. Benefits to be derived are several; each can participate and learn more about his or her personal issue without waiting for a turn, progress is more easily seen, and self-confidence can be enhanced when members see that whatever they produce is acceptable and of value in their therapy. Expressive processes can be very empowering for group members.

### Focus on Issues for the Group

During the life span of the group there may be instances when a member or the group-as-a-whole remains unaware of and resistant to acknowledging a problem or issue. The leader may find it more beneficial to let the group become aware of the resistance and issue through the expressive process rather than interpretation. Expressive processes can be used to promote awareness of both individual and group issues/concerns. Careful selection of a technique and adequate processing usually result in increased awareness and willingness to work on the matter.

### Highlights Universality

One of the eleven group therapeutic factors listed by Yalom (1985) is universality. When group members know that they are not the only ones to have a particular problem, concern, or issue, they feel less alone, less "wrong" or weird, and, begin to use the support resources present in the group. Simply telling about personal issues, concerns, or problems is not sufficient, as no two situations are the same and individuals resist accepting similarities because of perceived superficial differences. Expressive processes highlight the underlying and basic issues, problems, or concerns, and when this is done, similarities are more easily identified and accepted. The situations may differ but the issues, problems, or concerns are alike. This is where the expertise of the leader comes into play. Linking the elements together during processing helps to highlight similarities.

## EXAMPLES OF USES FOR EXPRESSIVE PROCESSES

Following are some commonly encountered problems or situations that lend themselves to use of expressive processes. These are not all inclusive but are representative of major concerns usually encountered in groups.

### Difficult Member Behaviors

There are some direct ways to address difficult behaviors and confronting is generally the most effective. However, until a therapeutic relationship is developed, trust is established in the group, safety issues are resolved, and the member is psychologically ready to receive the confrontation, other means, such as expressive processes, may produce the desired effect. Some examples follow.

### Monopolizing

An expressive technique or process may be especially useful with monopolizing behavior. The monopolizing behavior is usually verbal in nature, and expressive processes emphasize nonverbal ways of knowing. When it may be too early to confront the monopolizing behavior directly, a technique such as described in the chapter on fairy tales could be used. The behavior is thus interrupted, others have an opportunity to present and work on their issues, and the member who has been the center of attention receives no indication that his or her behavior has been a source of difficulty for the group. Other expressive processes could be used in the same way and for the same purpose.

### Hostility and Anger

When hostile, angry behavior is displayed that is difficult for the group to handle, and the individual displaying the behavior is not receptive or ready for confrontation, an imagery experience may be useful. Imagery used in this manner is a process that gives each member an opportunity to get in touch with his or her own hostile, angry feelings instead of only one member expressing those uncomfortable, undesirable feelings. An imagery exercise that teaches a method of containing and controlling these feelings would likely produce the desired effect. Further, the hostile angry member would not feel attacked or singled out as all members were participating. This, in and of itself, may produce better feelings of safety and cohesion within the group as well as for the particular member.

### Silent Member

Drawing, sculpting, or drama may be especially useful when trying to deal with a silent member. Instead of insisting that the person use words, these are other means for expressing what he/she is experiencing as well as providing other group members with alternative ways of expressing feelings or emotions. Sometimes, the more a silent member is pushed and encouraged to talk, the more he/she retreats. Expressive processes provide a means of participating that does not rely on words, and no one is put on the spot or "hot seat." By using expressive processes the silent member may feel more accepted for being what he/she is, and become more willing to speak up and interact with others.

### Story Telling

Story telling behavior can be blocked by the use of expressive processes. Instead of elaborating on details by one member, each member gets a chance to participate and interact. All of the expressive processes described in this book lend themselves to providing a means for group members to focus on their problems, issues, or concerns without the necessity for elaboration or details. The member doing the story telling does not feel cut off, as if he/she has talked too much or that others do not want to hear what they have to say.

### Problem Group Behaviors

Common problems that appear in groups that are shared by many or all members in the group can be troublesome at times, and efforts to resolve them become somewhat circular and frustrating. Members may unconsciously collude to continue the behaviors, and no amount of confronting seems to make a difference. Or, the needed awarenesses and behaviors that would address the problem are scary to members and so they continue to resist. Some of these persistent problem group behaviors are being unable to focus on feelings, dealing with intense emotions, resolving an impasse, and accepting personal responsibility.

### Inability to Focus on Feelings

In the beginning stages of group, many members may find it particularly difficult to focus on feelings. They tell stories, "talk about" feelings, and avoid or deny feelings and emotions. Group leaders try to counter this problem by modeling, reframing so as to focus on feelings and emotions, and directly confronting members with their avoidant or resistant behavior. The following model may help conceptualize what may be occurring in the group. The descriptions are for individuals but are also applicable to the group-as-a-whole. Understanding feelings as occurring in layers and as being dynamics makes it easier to determine what may be happening for individuals as well as the group.

## CONCEPTUALIZATION OF FEELINGS

### Feelings Occur in Layers

Elliott (1976) proposed a theory that feelings occur in layers and that superficial and overlying feelings have to be worked through before the underlying ones emerge. The discussion that follows uses parts of that assumption. Added to his assumption that feelings occur in layers are the premises that these layers are mostly not on the conscious level; that the layers are dynamic--moving, shifting, changing; and that defense mechanisms come into play at each level. The dynamics of feelings contribute to the difficulty in identifying and/or expressing feelings.

*Superficial layer*. The top level is termed *superficial* or *social* to reflect the primary function for behavior and feelings usually experienced. Behaviors characteristic of this level are politeness, rituals, there-and-then material, and "talking about" those feelings that are appropriate to the situation. The individual has on a social mask that seeks to conceal true feelings. Depending on the situation, feelings such as wariness, mild anxiety, or confidence are experienced. These are the kinds of feelings experienced at the beginning of a group when members are unsure what is expected of them, how they will be received by other members and the leader, and how they will react to others. However, they are seldom verbalized openly which would allow commonalities to be highlighted and fears addressed.

*Professional and Personal Demeanor layer*. The next layer is termed *professional and personal demeanor* and also reflects the function of tasks and contains feelings associated with everyday life and relationships: family, work, play, and so on. A certain amount of intimacy is present and individuals can allow some indication of what they feel they are really like to be shown to others. There is usually an awareness of not being fully open in expression of feelings but the superficial layer has been relaxed enough to allow some intimacy. Feeling and emotions experienced and expressed may remain a pale imitation of deeper ones, or some aspects of the deeper ones may be expressed. For example, affection may be expressed but also love; irritation but also anger. Defense mechanisms may still operate to protect self from more uncomfortable and unacceptable feelings and emotions. There is a great deal of masking of the intensity of feelings being experienced as well as repression and denial.

*Non-conducting layer*. When an individual is resisting or blocking intense feelings an insulating layer is in place. This layer is termed *non-conducting* as it protects the individual from experiencing or expressing these feelings and forms a barrier. Feelings and emotions expressed may be confusion, paralysis, blankness, or uncertainty. When asked what feelings are being experienced the individual may answer, "Nothing" or "I don't know." This layer can be present at any point. Some people may allow themselves to experience and express deeper and more intense emotions; their nonconducting layer is below those emotions. The non-conducting layer may also shift in response to a particular event or situation. That is if the individual feels threatened he/she will move the insulation layer closer to the top.

*Apprehension layer*. The worried, anxious, fearful layer can also appear in different places. This is the layer that contains feelings of unease around self issues and environmental concerns. Self issues of adequacy, competence, lovableness, and acceptance are examples. Environmental concerns are such considerations as potential evaluation and judgment by others, threat of attack, being ignored by others, not being understood, and being discounted. This level is termed *apprehension*.

*Being and non-Being layer*. Existential concerns characterize another layer, termed *being and non-being*. Characteristic feelings and emotions experienced are loneliness, alienation, dread, despair, and purposelessness. When feelings and emotions from this layer are experienced, they may be felt in indirect ways and expressed indirectly. For example, a group member may express dissatisfaction with his or her social life but not express dissatisfaction with feelings of isolation and alienation. He/she is not consciously aware that he/she is experiencing very basic feelings and emotions related to existential issues.

*Primary layer*. Primitive feelings and emotions such as anger, fear, guilt, and shame form a layer termed *primary*. These are very basic feelings and emotions experienced from infancy. They emerge as a response to a threat to the individual, either real or imagined. The older one is and the more negative experiences one has had, the more one has developed a sense that allows him or her to perceive threats in the present that are based on past experiencing. These feelings and emotions are very intense and can be experienced as overwhelming. Thus, group members may defend against experiencing or expressing anything from this primary layer for fear of hurting or destroying self or others. Some others may not know how to express milder forms of feelings on the primary layer and thus express none at all. Still others deny or repress that they ever experience these feelings at all.

*Dependence layer*. Feelings of worthlessness, helplessness, and yearning characterize the *dependence layer*. These feelings and emotions may be experienced temporarily or may be persistent. They may be chronic or acute. Many group members will be reluctant to admit having these feelings and emotions and, to protect themselves from experiencing these feelings, block others from expressing them. The extent of this layer is related to early experiences with others in infancy and childhood. The quality of primary relationships contributes to the degree to which this layer exists and how easily it is accessed.

*Actualized layer*. There is a final layer that is in different places for different people, the *actualized layer*. This layer contains feelings and emotions of self-liking and acceptance, competence, confidence, relatedness, and uniqueness. The person is differentiated, independent and interdependent, centered, balanced, self-directed, and autonomous: all the positive feelings and emotions about self that allow him or her to be open, accepting, and trusting of others.

### Resisting Experiencing Feelings

In addition to difficulties in focusing on feelings and emotions, some members will resist experiencing intense feelings and emotions and block others from experiencing them and/or dealing with them constructively. Intense feelings and emotions can be uncomfortable, threatening, and overwhelming. Individuals may feel that they have little or no control over being engulfed or consumed by them and so seek to avoid experiencing them. Others may be so threatened by the intensity that they block, repress, and deny them.

Whatever the reason for inability to focus on or deal with feelings and emotions, expressive processes can provide opportunities to do so in a relatively safe, nonthreatening way. For example, if several group members resist focusing on their anger or continue to block angry feelings an art activity that has them illustrate their anger could be used or one that has them use a color to draw a symbol for anger. Imagery may also be useful to help members focus on feelings, or sensations experienced prior to becoming angry. It then becomes possible to teach them how to intervene to prevent the feelings from escalating into overwhelming feelings and emotions.

### Group Issues

There are several common group issues that lend themselves to expressive processes, conflict, intimacy, dependency, and fears. These issues may be manifested differently at various stages of group development, and the expressive processes used can be adapted for stage of group development as well as emotional readiness of group members to participate at different stages. These common issues should be expected to be manifested in group and a leader can prepare in advance for using an expressive process to deal with them.

*Conflict.* Conflict arises early in group but is usually denied or unexpressed. When conflict becomes a block to the functioning of the group, it must be dealt with so that the group and members can move on. Conflicts occur between members and between members and the leader. If members continue to block, suppress, or deny conflict, a guided imagery that highlights members' characteristic way of dealing with conflict can be used. Once that is out in the open, the leader can guide or confront members to become aware of how they have been using their characteristic way of dealing with conflict in the group. When this has been expressed it becomes easier to begin to deal with conflict in the group more openly and constructively.

*Intimacy.* Intimacy is also a common issue that arises in group. Members have varying needs for intimacy as well as differing in their capacity to tolerate intimacy. This usually becomes a problem after the group has passed the getting acquainted stage. Some trust has developed, safety needs have been met to an extent that members feel comfortable, and members begin to explore relationships in the group. There may be resistance to intimacy in the group. Because of past experience members may be wary of being rejected, discounted, manipulated, or betrayed. They may be very aware that these past experiences are impacting the ability to develop meaningful relationships in the group, but are unable to change, or they may be unaware of the influences of past experiences. Either way, the group has reached an impasse and is not progressing.

Guided writing expressive processes described in Chapter 10 are designed to highlight past experiences that are influencing capacity for intimacy, and this "unfinished business" can be addressed.

Role play and drama are two processes that give opportunities to experiment with new behaviors which can increase capacity for, and comfort with, intimacy. Imagery can be used to explore possible benefits that could accrue from improved relationships within and outside the group if intimacy issues were better understood and resolved.

*Dependency.* Dependency issues, like intimacy issues, arise from previous experiences extending back to infancy. The need, desire, or yearning to gain approval, or to be taken care of, or the denial of these needs, when exhibited by several members can retard or impair the functioning of the group. A certain amount of regression is to be expected as members look to the leader to satisfy their needs. While it is the leader's responsibility to take care of some basic safety needs, some members demand more from the leader and the group. Indeed, an expected event in group, the attack on the leader, occurs when members are demanding in an open and vocal way that the leader take care of their needs.

Admitting that one has these needs, desires, yearnings is very difficult for some group members. They seem to feel that they must be entirely self-sufficient and that it is a sign of weakness and inadequacy to admit otherwise. Indeed, the leader may be the only one who verbalizes this need and may wish to explore it in indirect ways through use of an expressive process.

Among the expressive processes that lend themselves to focusing on and building awareness of dependency needs are fairy tales, drawing, and guided writing. Fairy tales that have dependency as one of their themes are an indirect way to highlight these needs and give hope that they can be accommodated or resolved. At the heart of dependency are the issues of separation and individuation which are addressed in several tales, such as "Hansel and Gretel," "Snow White," and "The Three Little Pigs."

Imagery experiences such as those described by Ahnsen (1977) are also useful. These imageries take you back to childhood experiences that focus on relationships with parents and other significant persons. The past is reexperienced and explored from the vantage point of the present, which highlights the impact of the past on current behavior or functioning.

Guided writing as described in Chapter 10 can also be used. It is a personal and private way to delve into your past and become more aware of issues and their antecedents. Fostering an awareness of dependency needs helps members to become more aware of how these needs may be impacting relationships in the group.

*Fears.* Fear of being known, of being rejected, of being perceived as "weird" or "wrong," of being hurt or destroyed, and of hurting or destroying others prevents members from expressing their feelings and emotions, and from being honest and open. These conditions have a negative influence on growth and development of the group. Adding to the complexity of fears is that the primary fear will differ among members. Selecting *an* expressive process will be very difficult, and the leader may have to plan to use more than one experience process or be able to identify the primary fear for the majority of group members.

Techniques selected could focus on feelings and emotions surrounding the basis for the fear, that is, being rejected: for example, an art activity that has a theme of feelings and emotions associated with rejection. A drawing of a situation illustrating rejection and a poem about rejection are other possibilities. Listing techniques one uses to avoid experiencing rejection or ways one continues to seek out rejecting situations and/or people is another example.

An issue for the group and leader that does not fall into the above categories is transference. Expressive processes that highlight previous relationships of members, especially parental relationships, can help members become aware of their transferences in the group.

## OTHER APPLICATIONS

### Pregroup Preparation

Expressive processes can provide prospective group members access to personal material and issues that are relevant for exploration in group sessions. Information derived is generally more focused, less confounded by group issues such as safety, and can be deeper and more significant, and less threatening.

For example, guided writing provides a relatively short way to review significants, such as events, relationships, works, in one's life with an emphasis on unfinished business. It is a personal and private way to engage in reflection in a group setting. New awarenesses emerge and can form the basis for even deeper analysis and understanding in later group sessions.

Other ways are to focus on communication and role play to teach relationships and communicating skills.

### Diaries and Journals

Members can be taught how to keep a daily diary or journal that will be helpful in the group. Suggest that they write each day about the day noting high points, low points, emotions experienced when doing ordinary and routine activities, periods of intense emotion, describe any situations generating intense emotions, and quality of relationships during the day. Patterns will emerge over time which provide more information about the person.

### Autobiographies

Writing an autobiography can be helpful for some members. Pregroup sessions that give structure and directions for the autobiography will usually keep them on task. For example, the first pregroup session can set the task, describe the process, and have them begin to write. For some, the progression of recall will not be in chronological order, and they will skip around time periods. Others will want to begin at the beginning and proceed chronologically to the present. Still others may wish to start at the present and proceed backward to earlier times. Members should be encouraged to complete the task in the way that makes sense to them and is easiest to complete.

It may be helpful to have members begin by listing major periods of their lives on separate sheets of paper, for example, childhood before entering school, kindergarten, and elementary school. Start with several periods spanning a relatively large time span. After listing ten to fifteen major periods, have them list any events they recall, people, and things such as toys, pets, or houses. Suggest that they consult photographs to prod memories. These lists form a framework for the autobiography, and the task is to use the lists to write about each period. It is probably most helpful if members use their personal memories at this point and not attempt to fill in the blanks by consulting others. They could be assigned periods to write about each week. Members who have difficulty remembering could use a notebook divided into time periods, and whenever they recall an event or other data, record it in the relevant section.

Blocked, repressed, or denied memories may emerge and do so in such a way that the person is ready to work on them. Unfinished business and its impact on current functioning become clearer and capable of being resolved or finished.

## EXPRESSIVE PROCESSES AS INTRODUCTIONS

### When the Group Begins

Any expressive process that is used at the beginning of a group should be quick, easy, and nonthreatening. The major, and possibly the only, objectives are to begin the introduction of members and to lower the anxiety level. Some simple art and/or music exercises make good icebreakers at the beginning of group. Imagery, fairy tales, guided writing, and drama may be too intense or threatening to members at this stage. Regardless of which expressive process is used, the emphasis is not on the product but on the primary purpose of getting acquainted.

### Name Tag Exercise

A variation of the name tag activity I have used in classes for many years would be to have members select one color felt tip marker, write the name by which they wish to be called in the group (this may be different from their given name or a nickname), and choose a symbol for their goal in the group. For example, a goal may be peace of mind and the symbol a dove; or, a better relationship with a loved one and the symbol clasped hands. If members say things like "I can't think of a symbol" or "I can't draw," encourage them to use any association they choose or just splashes of color. When they share the information on their name tags the meanings will be made clear.

**Musical Exercise**

Music can be selected to highlight or reduce tension usually present at the first session. Members listen quietly for two to three minutes and then respond to the statement, "Right now I'm feeling [or aware of]."

## EXPRESSIVE PROCESSES FOR SELF-EXPLORATION

**Self-awareness**

"Who am I?" is an ongoing exploration for group members. Becoming aware of repressed, suppressed, or denied memories; how they are perceived by others; and how they perceive themselves is a part of learning about self and relations to others. This is a very difficult process and resistance is sure to be encountered. Expressive processes are ideal for bypassing defenses, accessing relevant material, and producing new learning.

Before using an expressive process, the leader should be aware of the level of psychological maturity of group members and select activities that can be done in relative safety. In other words, do not select an activity that will plunge members into intense feelings and emotions that they are not ready to handle. If the leader uses homework assignments, some activities lend themselves to being worked on outside the group while others are more effective when completed in the group.

Imagery activities that focus on the inner self may be productive. For example, members can be guided to visualize their "social" self--the person or mask that they present to the world at large; their "intimate" self--the person revealed to family and close friends; their "inner" self as they perceive it--which may be shown to others or hidden from others. Members can draw the three "selves" or describe them.

Guided writing lends itself to helping members to explore themselves more deeply. The leader can select some aspect of self and have members explore it in more detail using the process described in Chapter 10.

An activity that I have used in class that has been effective for self-exploration is the "Book of Self." The book consists of an outline of important life events, photographs depicting a pictorial history or autobiography, a collage of values and attitudes, brief essays on selected existential issues (e.g. freedom and responsibility), and a poem or drawing that depicts some aspect of self felt to be important. There are many other processes that can be included in a Book of Self.

All expressive processes lend themselves to increasing the individual's awareness of and understanding about self. Some activities are more direct in accomplishing the objectives of awareness and understanding than others, but most can be adapted.

### The "Shadow" Side

Becoming aware of the shadow side of self and, more importantly, accepting it can be facilitated through expressive processes. While Jungian theorists refer to the *shadow*, other theorists may use terms and concepts like *disowned parts of self, fragmented self, repressed* and *denied characteristics*. However the unacceptable part(s) of self is described, coming to grips with and integrating these parts of self is a part of therapy. Some of the expressive processes described next were developed with the shadow side in mind.

### The Positive Side of "Shadow"

Have members make a list of ten to twelve positive attributes on a 5 x 8 card. If they get stuck and relationships in the group have developed to an acceptable level, other members can make suggestions. After this list has been constructed, instruct them to list the flip side of every positive attribute. The flip side represents a part of the shadow. Sharing and discussing reveal how these attributes are manifested in the person today. Open discussion helps to make these attributes less fearsome and individuals become more willing to accept that these are parts of them and can begin to focus on how to make changes if they wish to.

Another exercise is an imagery activity that directs members to visualize a person they dislike or are repelled by, and with whom they have a personal relationship--work, family, peers, and so on. While much could be learned from exploring attraction and repulsion of remote or fictional characters, this activity emphasizes real, personal relationships. A list of characteristics or behaviors that they dislike most about that person is generated. Lists can be shared at this point, or after the activity is further along.

Group activities such as those described also have the potential for promoting universality among group members. They may find that they are not alone in having the particular characteristic, again increasing acceptance of it.

### Termination

Most groups will have a definite life span and ending point. Appropriate termination can make use of expressive processes designed to have members get in touch with feelings and emotions around termination.

Some members may not have mastered giving constructive feedback and an art activity can provide the means for their doing so in order that significant or important information not be left uncommunicated. One activity involves homework, that of making a collage for each group member: collages of the experiencing, impressions, and awareness about the other person. Collages should have titles and enough time should be allowed so that members receive their collages, and have time to ask for clarification. I find that making this assignment at the beginning of group promotes attention to others and generates awareness of experiencing of others. Group members are eager to receive their collages and many put a lot of time and effort into constructing them and search for just the right picture or symbol to convey their thoughts.

Feelings around termination are often suppressed, denied, repressed, or displaced. Members collude to avoid talking about or experiencing these feelings. Bringing these feelings out into the open allows them to be dealt with in a direct, constructive way. An art activity derived and adapted from that described by Sourkes (1991) may be helpful. The description and directions are below.

Each member is provided with a large circle drawn on paper and a variety of broad felt tip pens, crayons, oil pastels, or chalk pastels. Every person needs to have access to a variety of colors. The leader has constructed a list of feelings and emotions usually associated with termination, eight to twelve words or phrases. Members are instructed to select one color, and fill in an area in the circle that corresponds to the extent or intensity of their feeling or emotion about termination. For example, one word may be *sad,* and some members may experience a little sadness, while other members may admit to a great deal of sadness. One member would color in a small area and the other, a much larger one. The size and shape are left up to the individual.

These are only a few examples of applications of expressive processes is group counseling. Others are presented in later chapters and readers are encouraged to develop their own unique expressive processes.

# 7

# ART

## APPLICATIONS AND PROCESS FOR ART ACTIVITIES

### Rationale

Art activities can be very useful in group counseling, primarily because they do not rely on words to express feelings and emotions, or ambiguous or vague concepts when communicating with others. There are times when words are inadequate, unavailable, or used to conceal, and art activities provide additional means for expression. There are also individuals with low verbal skills who must struggle to express their thoughts, feelings and emotions, attitudes, opinions, and so forth. It's not that they do not want to--they just don't have adequate vocabularies or skills. Art activities allow for a different mode for expression of feelings for these individuals. Art can also serve as a mode of response when using other expressive processes such as imagery and fairy tales.

There are numerous varieties of art activities, each with its own unique advantages; however, this discussion will focus on only a few. These were selected because they can be described easily, can be completed by almost anyone, are not overly time consuming, and have been shown to be useful in therapy. There are other art activities that also meet these criteria and the reader is encouraged to seek them out. A distinct advantage for the presented art activities is the usability in group counseling. Each has been used and found to facilitate group progress. The selected art activities also have the advantage of being simple to execute by the leader and require no artistic ability or training as an art therapist. It is helpful if the leader has had experience and/or training, but an interest in these kinds of activities and an understanding of how they facilitate group and members progress are sufficient.

Art therapists, on the other hand, do have to have extensive formal training. These are professionals who can interpret art products. Their use of art activities is very different from that described in this book. They are trained professionals who can make in-depth analyses, which are far beyond that which is proposed herein. The procedures and process described in this chapter focuses on using art activities as alternative means of expressing feelings and emotions, thoughts, opinions, and so on, rather than totally relying on words.

## GUIDELINES

### Goals and Objectives

The leader must have a clearly defined objective before initiating an art activity. Participation is enhanced when group members have some knowledge of why the activity is proposed and what benefits they are supposed to derive. For example, an art activity used at the first group session may have the objective of helping members to become acquainted in a more focused way than just telling name, occupation, and so on. A well planned simple art activity can help members disclose more relevant and personal information appropriate at the first meeting, and facilitates the process whereby members become acquainted, begin to see similarities, and establish relationships.

There are two main components of an objective or goal for using art activities: benefit for the group and for individual members. Both should be remembered when developing the reason to introduce the activity: what benefits can accrue to the group-as-a-whole and what benefit(s) for individuals can be anticipated. It is not productive to do an activity just to do one or if only one or two members are expected to learn, understand, or benefit in some way. This does not mean that everyone needs to have the same issue or problem before an art activity can be used; it does mean that most group members can relate to the issue or problem in some way. For example, in a group of young adults, some married and some not married, introducing an art activity focusing on marital issues or problems would not be relevant for all group members or for the group-as-a-whole. However, focusing on problems or issues with intimacy in relationships would involve all members as well as addressing a group issue.

### Choosing an Activity

Activities should be chosen after careful consideration of the time available, stage of group development, and members' psychological readiness. Some activities can be adapted or modified to be used in different ways and all or most stages of development, while others have limited use. Paying attention to these criteria will contribute to effective and productive outcomes.

*Time Available*. The primary emphasis for any expressive process is on guiding members to increase awareness of personal reactions and associations, not on creating. It is easy to get caught up in construction of a product and lose sight of the primary objective or intention of the experience. For these reasons art activities should be selected to be easily completed by all group members in a short period. Art expressive processes have a greater impact if construction and processing are completed in the same session. Time constraints will rule out using many worthwhile art activities and the leader must balance possible therapeutic benefits of an extensive art activity against the therapeutic needs of the group.

*Stage of Group Development.* Activities produce different outcomes and have different constraints depending on the stage of group development. Activities appropriate for the working stage may be too threatening if used in the getting acquainted stage. On the other hand, an activity may be used to get acquainted and used again in a later stage in another way with very different outcomes. For example, the color wheel (described later in this chapter) could be used in an early session to help members express feelings and emotions about being in a group, for example, fear. The same activity could be used in the transition from the working stage to the terminating stage for highlighting feelings and emotions around separating and loss.

*Psychological Readiness.* Introducing an art activity, or any expressive process, before members are psychologically ready to handle the affect generated is counterproductive to development of the therapeutic relationship, trust, and safety for group members. Too much too soon will leave members scared and resistant--just what the activity was trying to overcome. Knowing when to introduce tension, and how much tension will be constructive, is learned over time and with experience. Too little is better than too much. Members need to trust the leader to care for their safety needs, and, when members feel safe, they are more likely to lower defenses and work to overcome resistances. The leader must stay alert to the depth and intensity of affect aroused for members.

**Materials**

*Description.* Art activities demand that sufficient materials be available. It is most desirable for each member to have his or her own set of equipment with which to work, for example, felt tip markers, but some can be shared between two or three members. The leader has the responsibility of gathering materials before the session begins so that none of the group's time is wasted.

Group leaders who want to use art expressive processes may wish to keep basic materials on hand. Suggested basic materials are newsprint 12 x 18 or larger, eight to ten sets of fine and broad felt tip markers, eight to ten pairs of paper cutting scissors, glue sticks, masking tape, construction paper, boxes of assorted crayons, old magazines and catalogues with lots of pictures, and different colors of a nonhardening clay product. Additional optional materials are sets of oil and chalk pastels, tissue paper for collages, charcoal, fixative, colored pencils, white drawing paper, hardening clay, and acrylic paints and glazes for the clay. It is a good idea to have premoistened paper towels on hand for cleaning up after using chalk and clay. Materials should be easily accessible and suitable for the age and educational level of participants.

The group leader should become familiar with the properties of art materials in order to choose those that enhance the expressive process. For example, crayons come in a wider variety of colors than do felt tips. However, crayons do not glide color on paper as easily as felt tips. Having to work harder at coloring a surface may take away attention from what is being experienced. Attention may switch from internal experiencing to the product. Another example is the difference in intensity of colors produced by oil pastels and chalk pastels. The colors of oil pastels are deeper and more brilliant than those of chalk pastels. Chalk, charcoal, and clay or clay products leave residues on the hands and spread easily so that products can become readily smudged.

### Procedures

*Introduction.* Introduce an art activity by explaining the objective for the experience, such as getting acquainted or expressing feelings and emotions nonverbally. If there is an impasse or another difficulty in the group, point out that talking hasn't helped and you want to try another way.

*Description.* Describe the activity briefly: for example, "I will give an emotion and ask you to select one color and draw a symbol for it." Do not overexplain but give enough information so that group members have some idea what to expect and can better concentrate on their inner experiencing. This is also the point where members can ask clarifying questions and receive reassurances.

Emphasize that creating a product (e.g., a drawing) is important but that the quality of the product is immaterial. Many members will hesitate to participate because they fear ridicule or rejection of their product as inadequate or without artistic merit. Participation in some activities can be encouraged if the leader shows the group some typical products. It is useful to gather some examples of products developed by members in previous groups, taking care not to have any identifying data on them.

*Encouragement to Participate.* Encourage members to participate but do not demand that they do so. Forced participation arouses resistances that may be difficult or impossible to overcome. Encouragement is also given by the leader's nonjudgmental acceptance. This means that the leader must take care not to make positive comments such as, "That is very good," as well as not making negative comments. Neutral comments such as, "You are working very hard," or "You seem to be stuck, can I help?" are examples of encouragement to participate. If the leader feels a compliment is warranted, it should be given after all processing is completed. Members should have no doubts about the suitability and acceptability of their products. The leader should also be alert to blocking inappropriate comments by other group members.

### Processing

Allow time for members to display and tell something about their products. Members may finish at different rates and may be encouraged to post their products, if they are drawings, on the wall with masking tape and to look at each other's products. Requesting members to briefly describe their products clarifies some associations for them. This part of processing should be interrupted as little as possible because following up and deepening the experience for one member may not leave enough time for all members to relate their experiences. Further, opportunities for linking may be overlooked or lost. Instead of interrupting, the leader can make notes to him or herself to return to a particular point or person.

*Focus on Feelings and Emotions.* As members relate their experiences, the leader should keep the focus on feelings and emotions that were aroused and/or are current. Doing so allows the leader to better gauge the level and intensity of affect around the experience. If feelings and emotions are intense, then the leader can make sure that the member or members is(are) not overwhelmed by the intensity, assist in clarifying, and give support on working through the emotions. If feelings and emotions appear to be superficial, the leader can formulate questions and comments to deepen the experience or highlight resistances. All provide valuable material with which to work.

Some general questions I have found to be helpful are, "What feelings and/or emotions were aroused as you did the activity?" "What feelings, emotions, or awarenesses do you have now?" "What was difficult?" "Easy?"

*Psychological State of Members.* Each activity may have a different set of specific inquiries. These are also dependent on the psychological state of the group members. That is, are they prepared or strong enough to deal with any sensitive or emotionally laden material that can emerge? It does little good to ask a penetrating question that pushes the member into an emotional state that he/she cannot adequately handle. This situation may be compounded by the person's covering up or hiding the degree of distress so well that the leader cannot detect it. Another consideration is the group's ability to deal with the query or comment. While the member to whom it is directed may be able to handle it effectively, other members may be less able to do so. The leader has the responsibility to take care of the group as well as its individual members. It is preferable to be restrained in the processing of expressive activities when there is little certainty, knowledge or understanding of the psychological state of group members.

*Level and Intensity of Involvement.* Ask the individual presenting the product about the extent to which he/she was, and is, involved in construction or creating that work. The answer is another indication of the significance of the activity for the person. A superficial involvement may signal resistance to personal material or a reluctance based on the activity itself. Further exploration usually indicates which applies. If it is resistance to personal material, accept it for now and do no further exploration unless that member initiates it. Go back to it in another session. If the activity itself was a hindrance to participation, ask whether there are others who feel the same way, and try to determine what there was about the activity that precipitated their reluctance. The answers may provide information that leads to successful modification of the activity or additional information about the members. For example, I used a finger painting activity in a graduate class on counseling children once to illustrate a means of releasing creativity, reexperiencing a childhood state, and having fun. To my chagrin, there were several adults who did not like doing the activity although the vast majority had a good time. These feelings came out during processing and the primary reason given was that they had a strong aversion to getting dirty or messy. One person recalled that she always felt her finger painting products in kindergarten were inferior to others and had never liked to engage in it since that time. While this would be good material to explore in counseling, this was a class, and since I cannot screen students for the class, I eliminated that experience and substituted another one.

*New Awarenesses*. The leader will wish to know whether members gained any awareness, learning, or understanding about themselves or their relationships. This should be a direct query. Having members verbalize this information somehow makes it more real or relevant for them. They become more willing to explore it, make associations, and, in some cases, view it from another perspective. Care must be taken not to demand that members gain anything from doing the activity. Some may not gain, some may gain only a fragment, others may feel left out or different from other members if they cannot say that they gained something, and still others may fabricate a response in an attempt to please the leader. The leader must accept that little or nothing happened for that member and not suggest that it was a result of resistance, even if it is obvious that the member was resisting.

## ART ACTIVITIES AND STAGES OF GROUP DEVELOPMENT

### Initial Stage

The beginning sessions of group are characterized by confusion, milling around, and anxiety. Members are unsure about being in a group, may not know what to expect or what is expected of them, fear the unknown, have unspoken safety and trust issues, want to be taken care of by the leader, and are wary of fellow group members. The situation is new, the people are new, roles may be new, and activities are new. The leader has the responsibility of addressing all of these concerns as well as helping members to work on personal issues, all of which may be different.

Art activities can facilitate working through all of these concerns/problems in a timely manner, and has the added advantage of being relatively non-threatening for members. The leader can focus on primary concerns, highlight and make known feelings that members are experiencing, and promote confidence in each member's personal ability to handle whatever emerges in the group as well as confidence in the leader and other members. Carefully selected art activities can address issues members may not be aware of or able to articulate. The leader knows that these are common issues that are expected to emerge in the initial stage and can plan to help members increase their awarenesses and address them in a satisfactory way.

Generally, art activities selected for this stage should be short, easily completed by all members, and nonthreatening, in both construction and amount of information revealed. Objectives, at this point, are focused on decreasing anxiety, promoting feelings of safety and trust, and providing enough knowledge of group members to underscore universality, encourage hope, and provide some interpersonal learning. Several such activities are described. The descriptions will also provide suggestions for adaptations for children.

*Name Tags*. Fold 5 x 8 index cards in half lengthwise and have group members write their name, or what they want to be called, on it together with a symbol they associate with themselves. Each member then tells what the symbol stands for and one other piece of information he or she wants to share with the group. A modification would be to use name tags that can be pinned or stuck on instead of index cards. The leader may wish to prepare his or hers in advance as an example. No modification is needed for children.

Materials are index cards (5 x 8) or name tags, felt tip markers in a variety of colors.

*Getting to know me*. Group members are given a blank sheet of paper (8 ½ x 11 or larger), and a set of colored markers: felt tips, crayons, oil pastels, or pencils. The leader asks them to divide their paper mentally into four quadrants and to draw a symbol in each using only one color for each symbol. Four different colors may be used but only one color per symbol. The leader then slowly gives the directions for symbols. In the first quadrant draw a symbol for "something you have done that makes you proud." In the second, a symbol for "something you find hard to do." In the third, a symbol for "something you would like to learn to do," and in the fourth, a symbol for "a current emotion you are experiencing." After each one allow enough time for members to draw their symbols.

Alternatives are a favorite possession; music, sport, or hobby they participate in; and most liked activity.

For children select any four things that would appeal to them, such as a toy, a school subject, what they are proud of about themselves, and most liked thing.

This is also an exercise that can be effectively used in later stages of group. For example, it could be used at termination to focus on how members perceived their experience in the group.

Materials are paper and colored markers.

*Expressions of Me*. The leader should have a box of cut out pictures. Use pictures from catalogues, magazines, and so on. Ask group members to select two to three pictures they feel express something about themselves that they would like to share with other members. Emphasize that what is expressed should be something of importance not usually shared with strangers.

This exercise could also focus on feelings around conditions, such as an eating disorder, or other issues that are known to be common to group members as the group is formed.

Materials are cut out pictures and a box or boxes.

*Collages*. The leader can decide on the topic for a collage such as self, values, or current functioning. Members are asked to construct a collage that expresses their perceptions of the topic.

Materials are construction paper, a variety of catalogues and magazines, glue, felt markers, and masking tape.

With children the leader can save time by providing members with a box of cut out pictures from which they can choose.

*Drawings*. A variation of the use of collages described is to have group members draw instead of constructing a collage. Have them draw a picture of self, of a value they hold dear, of how they feel they are functioning well or not well at this point. Almost any topic that is related to the group and getting to know group members is appropriate as long as care is taken not to select a topic that calls for overly deep self-disclosure at this point.

Materials are large sheets of newsprint, markers and masking tape.

### Stage 2 - Conflict and Control

When the group reaches stage 2, members are less polite and more open about conflict and control. They may not express these directly, but they are not as well hidden as they are during stage 1. This is the time when members are more apt to express irritation or anger, challenge the leader, and exhibit problem behaviors. Open expression and discussion of conflict can lead to resolution; however, many times expression of conflict is covert and indirect, making it difficult to deal with it effectively because of unacknowledged feelings and emotions. Art activities can highlight what members and the group-as-a-whole are experiencing and make feelings and emotions that are under the surface or hidden more open and direct.

It is not unusual for group members to suppress uncomfortable emotions such as anger. They may be unaccepting of their own anger and of that expressed by others. The entire group may collude to ensure that anger remains hidden and unexpressed. Some members may deny having angry feelings and/or be so fearful of becoming overwhelmed or rejected that they act as if the anger did not exist. These uncomfortable feelings and emotions are usually connected or related to conflict in the group as well as relationships outside the group and contribute to actions that seek to hide or deny that there is conflict. It can be very beneficial to individual members and to the group to facilitate expression and resolution of conflicts in the group setting. Further, the activities can help teach members how to appropriately express uncomfortable or intense feelings.

When a leader realizes that members are impeding group progress by denying or suppressing expression of uncomfortable feelings, he/she can use an art activity designed to help members appropriately express these feelings, make the nature of the conflict more open and direct, and highlight awareness of associations for members on suppression of feelings and of conflicts for relationships inside and outside the group. If group members lack skills to express these emotions appropriately and/or awareness of gradations, art activities can also be used to teach skills and awareness.

*Feelings and Emotions Book.* The feelings and emotions book activity would be useful to promote awareness of gradations of feelings and emotions, and to develop ways to express them appropriately. It could be used as a homework exercise as it would take several sessions to complete, assuming that only one set of feelings and emotions for example, love, is discussed in a session.

The leader should identify the feelings and emotions to be highlighted. Common ones are anger, sadness, guilt, shame, love, happiness, resentment, and inadequacy. There are numerous others and these can also be used. Each feeling or emotion comprises one chapter in the book. Chapters contain drawings, a collage, and a brief paragraph or essay about the feeling and emotion. Members are asked to draw a symbol for the feeling and/or emotion. The leader may wish to limit the color choice to only one. More than one symbol can be drawn but each should be on a separate page. Another drawing would be of a situation when the person experienced the feeling or emotion. The collage would focus on situations, events, and people associated with their experiencing of the feeling and emotion. The paragraph or essay would address one of the following topics: physical sensations experienced during the feeling or emotion, such as blushing when experiencing shame; difficulties in expressing it; impact on relationships outside the group; fears, consequences, and impact on the group for openly expressing or not expressing the feeling or emotion.

As each set is completed, chapters are compiled and members can add items such as photographs, additional drawings, and poems. Focusing on those emotions that are blocking group progress allows them to be discussed openly in a nonthreatening way.

Materials used are paper, 8 ½ x 11 or 9 x 12 (the paper for all these projects should be the same size); felt tip markers, oil pastels, and/or chalk pastels, glue, and a variety of magazines.

*Feeling wheel.* Sourkes (1991) used a feeling mandala with pediatric oncology patients and their siblings. A modified version, termed a feeling wheel, is described for use at this stage to help members express feelings that are being suppressed, around a conflict with members and/or the leader. Prior to initiating the activity, the leader should compile a list of eight to ten feelings and emotions around the conflict. Focus on denied, suppressed, and/or unexpressed feelings and emotions that are having a negative impact on the group's progress. For example, if members are reluctant to express anger or irritation with the leader, a list can be drawn up to contain feelings and emotions, such as dependence, irritation, helplessness, anger, inadequacy, rejection, acceptance, powerlessness, revenge, and affection. Lists can be compiled for common feelings and emotions around certain issues.

Give each member a sheet of paper on which a large circle has been drawn, and a set of colored markers such as crayons, felt tip markers, oil pastels, or chalk pastels. Each member should have access to a variety of colors.

Tell members that a list of feelings and emotions will be read slowly. As they are named, a color should be selected and a portion of the circle filled. The amount of space used and the shape should be reflective of the level and intensity of the experienced feeling or emotion in the group, or around a particular situation or event in the group. Members may also add any feelings or emotions they experienced that were not on the list. The leader could have one or two examples prepared that showed differing shapes and colors in the wheel, not just even pie shapes.

This exercise needs little or no adaptation for use with children except to use words that are common that children in their age group are expected to know and use.

Materials are paper with large circles drawn on and sets of colored markers such as crayons, felt tip markers, oil pastels, and chalk pastels.

*Draw a conflict.* The draw-a-conflict activity can have any one of three emphases; intrapersonal, interpersonal, or group-as-a-whole. The directions would be based on which was being emphasized. After passing out materials, the leader gives directions, for example, "Draw symbols, or a situation, that illustrates a current or ongoing intrapersonal conflict." Processing would focus on having members define and clarify the conflict: describe payoffs for self and others; barriers to resolving the conflict, such as self, others, or situations; and the emotions, old messages, and associations around the conflict and drawing.

Materials are large sheets of newsprint, markers and masking tape.

### Stage 3

After conflict has surfaced, been acknowledged, and worked through, members enter what has been termed the "working stage." It is at this point that they have developed enough feelings of trust and safety that they can begin to reveal parts of themselves that heretofore they sought to conceal. Some may be ready to examine parts of self seen by others but unseen by them. While guilt and shame continue to play a part in resistance, members become more willing to lower defenses for a closer examination and deeper exploration of self. Few expressive activities are needed at this stage and an over reliance on use of them may interfere rather than help. Group leaders may want to reserve use of activities for when the group has reached an impasse or when there is tension.

An impasse usually occurs when many, most, or all group members are suppressing intense important feelings and emotions. The group appears to spin its wheels and discussions become circular. The feelings and emotions may be suppressed because they are too threatening; members may fear rejection, hurting others, destruction of the cohesion built in the group, or loss of control. The leader needs to have some sense of what fears may be causing an impasse before initiating an activity. Impasses may be the group's way of asking for reassurance that it is safe to express these feelings, they will be taken care of if they express them, and expression will not destroy them, the leader, other group members, and/or the group.

There are also occasions when the group has confronted a deep, intense emotional experience and members become stuck in the tension. An expressive activity could help relieve the tension and take members back to a more comfortable state.

*Collaborative Drawing.* Divide the group into dyads or triads with one large sheet of paper per subgroup. Each subgroup also receives a set of colored markers. The leader's directions are to draw a picture without talking to each other. As members draw, the leader should observe whether they took turns, each worked on a separate section, or all built on each other's contribution, as well as facial and body expression.

Processing should focus on feelings that emerged as they worked together and what it was like to have to develop a drawing without talking to each other. How they chose to draw can also be explored.

Materials are paper 11 x 15 or larger; colored markers such as crayons, colored pencils, felt markers, oil pastels, or chalk pastels; and masking tape.

*Finish the Drawing.* This works best if members stand to do it. Each group member receives a large sheet of paper and is instructed to select *one* color from the set of crayons, felt tip markers, or oil pastels. The activity begins with each member's making a mark on his or her paper. At a signal from the leader, each moves to the next person's sheet of paper and using the same color, adds to the mark(s) in any way he/she chooses. The group continues to move and mark until they have returned to their original paper. At this time they may complete their drawing, still using the same color. The final step is to give the drawing a title. Drawings are posted and discussed. The leader should be alert to how members feel about what emerged as their drawing, and any associations to current functioning or experiencing. Often the drawing done by the group for an individual produces a product that has relevant associations for that person's life. This is one reason for the leader to make sure to ask whether this is the case for any member.

Materials are a large sheet of paper for each member, one set of colored markers with enough different colors so that each member can select a distinctive one, and masking tape.

### Stage 4

Leaders need to plan for termination, whether the group is open, with members leaving and new members entering; closed, with members leaving and no new ones accepted; or time-bound, with a specified number of sessions.

Leaders should also plan what they would do if there is premature termination by a member.

Termination tends to arouse old feelings and emotions around issues of loss and abandonment. Members resist dealing with termination by denying conflicting feelings and emotions, refusing to deal with the topic exemplified by changing the subject, or taking flight into the future. Fears that there will not be enough time for their concerns cause members to shut down and begin to withdraw. Art activities can provide a means for members to express these complex feelings and emotions as well as an opportunity to finish working on issues that may have emerged during the group.

*Collages*. The collage activity can be assigned about halfway through the group sessions. This would allow enough time for members to feel comfortable with the leader and to know something about other members. The objective would be to have a mechanism for members to give each other feedback on their personal perceptions of each other, and to provide an opportunity for members to communicate feelings and emotions before termination.

Each member is asked to construct a collage for each of the other group members. These collages would have the theme of communicating personal feelings, emotions, and perceptions of the other. These may have been stated directly; however, many times members feel that the opportunity to say some things to each other was missed and the collages help recapture that opportunity.

The leader can allow enough time during the last sessions for members to share collages and clarifications.

If this exercise is used with children a session should be set aside for construction of collages and one to talk about them. It may be too complex to give as homework for children.

Materials, can be supplied by members, including paper or poster board, magazines, glue, and other items that symbolize feelings, emotions, and perceptions such as shells, buttons, and dried flowers.

*The Unseen Self.* The next activity is a variation on the Johari Window. The *Johari Window* concept proposes that there are four sections of self: the part seen by self and others, the part seen by self but not by others, the part seen by others but not by self, and the part seen neither by self nor by others. The art activity is a collaborative collage for each member, focusing on the part of self seen by others but not seen by self.

Provide a sheet of construction paper or poster board for each person and a variety of magazines, colored markers, and glue. The leader instructs members to find symbols to represent a part of each member that they have perceived and are not sure the member is aware of or have reason to believe that the person may be unaware. Each member is to contribute at least one symbol for each of the other group members. Enough time should be allowed for collages to be constructed and discussed.

Materials are construction paper or poster board, a variety of magazines, scissors, colored markers, and glue.

*A Group Mural.* The group is asked to plan and construct a mural that reflects perceptions, feelings, and emotions about the group.

Materials are scissors, construction paper in a variety of colors, colored markers, glue, and a 48 x 36 or larger piece of heavy white cardboard.

### Premature Termination

Premature termination arouses intense feelings in group members who may not understand why the member left so precipitously. Remaining members are confused about what their role was in the termination, whether the group is now unsafe for them, and some may fear being let down one more time. Leaders have a great deal of work to do in the group when a member leaves before the group ends, or before there has been closure. All of the art activities described previously that focus on identification and expression of feelings are appropriate.

# 8

# IMAGERY

## IMAGERY AS AN EXPRESSIVE PROCESS

### Definitions and Description

Reveries, daydreams, imagery, and fantasy are very similar in many ways. *Reverie* is defined as "dreamy thinking or imagining, especially of agreeable things." *Daydreams* are "pleasant, dreamy thoughts." *Imagery* is "forms of the fancy; mental images" and *fantasy* is "in psychology, a mental image, as in a daydream, usually pleasant and with some vague continuity" (*Webster's Dictionary* 1983). *The Dictionary of Psychotherapy* (Walrond-Skinner 1986) defines imagery as "the inner representation of objects and events created at will by the conscious mind." Many therapists have made use of imagery in therapy, although their terms and uses differed.

Imagery was used by Freud in therapy for a period, but he shifted to using free association instead of imagery. Jung (1960) termed the form of guided imagery he used *active imagination*. Desoille (1966) developed the *directed daydream*. His technique involved suggested actions, events, or objects injected into the imagining. Leuner (1969) called his method *guided affective imagery*, Assagioli (1965) used a variety of guided imagery techniques which he termed *psychosynthesis,* and Ahnsen's (1977) *eidetic imagery* conceptualizes the individual's original experiences to be filed in the psyche as eidetic visual units. These eidetic visual units can be retrieved through guided imagery. Each original experience is recorded in the psyche with three components: an image that portrays a situation, a somatic state composed of body feelings and the emotions attached to the image, and meaning of the image. The process of visualization is under the individual's control which is one way imagery differs from drawing.

Imagery, especially guided imagery, can be conceptualized as the spontaneous unedited reaction in symbolic form to external *cues* during a waking state. Although eyes are closed to better see or focus on the images, the person is awake the entire time and, most importantly, in conscious control of the images. Imaging can be stopped at any time by simply opening one's eyes.

### Therapeutic Uses of Imagery

The many theories, definitions, and uses of imagery contribute to understanding how, when, and where it can be used to further the therapeutic process. Some examples follow.

Jung (1960) used imagery and dream work for diagnostics and as techniques for achieving integration and individuation. He introduced the idea of the therapist's allowing the client or patient to derive the meaning of images instead of interpreting for him or her. Prior to this, it was felt that only the therapist had the "correct interpretation" and it was his or her responsibility to suggest, manipulate, or force acceptance of that interpretation. Jung felt that images have personal associations for the individual and the therapist could not possibly know what these associations were. Although he also used interpretations from the "collective unconscious," be considered personal associations to be important.

Gestalt therapists use imagery to promote awareness and understanding of disowned parts of self. Imagery is also used to uncover fears and expectations and make them more open so that they can be confronted and dealt with constructively. Polster and Polster (1973) list four functions of imagery: to get in touch with resisted events, feelings, or personal characteristics; to uncover unfinished business and complete it; to explore unknown future events; and to explore heretofore unknown parts of self.

### Physical Healing

Rossman (1993) uses guided imagery extensively in his medical practice as a way of helping patients to cope better with and self-manage illnesses, diseases, and chronic conditions. He lists two ways that guided imagery is used in health care, actively and receptively: *actively* by using imagery to alleviate symptoms, and *receptively* by allowing images to emerge as a means of understanding the emotional meanings of symbols. He describes three ways imagery is useful in mind/body medicine and healing: by producing physiological changes, psychological insight, and emotional awareness.

Many physicians and other health care professionals are using imagery to help patients alleviate pain, manage symptoms and promote healing. For a more complete overview of how imagery is used for physical healing see Consumer Reports (1990).

### Behavior Rehearsal

Guided imagery is also useful to help prepare members for a future event by leading them through a visualization, such as a behavior rehearsal. This is another form of role play except that it takes place for all group members at the same time. Guided imagery may be particularly useful by helping members gain confidence and belief in their competencies.

### Advantages of Guided Imagery

Among the special advantages of guided imagery are the following:

*Imagery bypasses defenses*: Imagery occurs on a nonverbal or preverbal level, and, as in dreams, symbolic representations of significants emerge. Individuals tend not to feel threatened by the images they generate, and this allows defenses to be lowered or bypassed.

*Imagery is relatively nonthreatening*: Meanings of images are not immediately apparent and additional work is needed to understand them. Therefore, a considerable amount of highly significant material can emerge because the individual does not feel in danger from the material.

*Imagery exercises tend to reconnect people to the deeper processes in their lives*: Imagery is going on inside people all the time. Unstructured imagery exercises can help them become connected to this process so they feel more centered and grounded, more in touch with their rich inner world, less needful of external support. Sometimes people are surprised to discover that images have a lot of energy. This energy can be released by contacting the images, giving them room to unfold, and can serve as the basis for new directions in a person's life. People become more focused and motivated, so that positive accomplishments seem to happen by themselves, demanding no extraordinary applications of will-power or self-discipline.

*Imagery work helps people to become more spontaneous and creative*: A new dimension of enjoyment is added to all activities when people begin to react spontaneously to life events with imagery as well as thoughts. Imagery opens up new areas of feeling which makes life richer and more zestful.

## INDICATIONS FOR USE IN GROUP WORK

Banet and Jones (1976) give the following conditions for using guided imagery:

*Resolve dilemmas or work through an impasse*: When verbal transactions are garbled, discussion becomes repetitive, or unvoiced fears stifle process, a guided imagery can usually produce fresh data and new solutions. A well designed imagery exercise can help member refocus or reframe so as to see the dilemma or impasse from a different perspective.

*Tap deeper layers or levels*: Discussion centering around difficult topics, such as authority, sexuality, or aggression, often stays at a superficial level. Guided imagery can move the discussion to a more meaningful level, as well as sanction the expression of difficult feelings.

*Focus or personalize learning*: Generalized verbal discussion frequently becomes anonymous. Guided imagery promotes ownership and personalized learning.

*Play*: In group therapy discussions frequently become unnecessarily serious, especially when group members are highly task oriented. Guided imagery provides a respite from work and can produce new data.

*Promote creativity*: Guided imagery frequently helps group members to uncover their originality and gain freshness of perception.

*Promote healing*: Disruptions, conflict, and interpersonal wounds can often be transposed to an allegoric or metaphoric level and resolved.

*Provide cues for intervention*: The facilitator will often find it useful to check in with his or her own ongoing experience to sharpen the reading of group process and to search for cues for appropriate interventions.

## TYPES OF GUIDED IMAGERY

Guided imageries can be classified into five categories, narrative, free form, interactive and metaphoric. All, except interative, are relatively easy to use in a group. Materials are also easy to find or develop. Leaders will find it helpful to gather a variety of imagery exercises, some specific themes and others more open ended, to have available when needed.

### Narrative

Content in narrative guided imagery is specified by the facilitator through frequent cues and interruptions in the process. The structure may be a classic form (e.g., a well-known fairy tale or story) or a simple scenario invented by the facilitator. The facilitator determines the course of the imagery by suggestions and specific directions.

### Free-form

Content is largely determined by the participant(s) in free-form guided imagery. Facilitators may present minimal initial cues (words, pictures, sounds, etc.) but leave gaps of silence that participants fill with their personal productions. Words or cues used are more abstract to allow for a wider variety of respones or images.

### Interactive

Interactive guided imagery enables participants to speak or move while engaged in the process. Many gestalt techniques involve such interaction, where occasionally the process is interrupted, and there is some verbal interaction between the imaginer and the facilitator. This can also be used in a group where members will speak aloud their images, at different times, and the leader makes suggestions. This form of guided imagery is very difficult to do effectively and considerable training in its use needed.

### Metaphoric

These guided imageries use fairy-tale characters and supranormal feats and activities, with the participant as an actor involved in the story or is an observer. For example, members could be Jack or the giant in the fairy tale "Jack in the Beanstalk."

## GUIDELINES FOR USING GUIDED IMAGERY IN A SESSION

Imagery exercises work better for the group if the leader follows the few simple guidelines listed below. These appear to be useful even when group members are familiar with guided imagery and have prior experiences. It is strongly recommended that guided imagery not be used in the first group session unless all members have had considerable experience with it. Members need to feel safe and have confidence in the leader's ability to protect them before engaging in guided imagery.

Plan to introduce a guided imagery activity to accomplish a purpose. The leader should ask him or herself, "What awarenesses would be gained by using a guided imagery?"

Select an exercise that appears to be suitable for the purpose. If participants are new to guided imagery, it may be useful to begin with a short non-threatening guided imagery such as, "Visualize a rose. What kind of rose is it? What color? Where is the rose?" After processing this one, more significant ones can be introduced.

Introduce the imagery exercise by *asking* members' permission to try one. *Never* impose an imagery exercise. If there is resistance to the idea, it is more useful to explore feelings and thoughts around the resistance than it is to forge ahead with the exercise.

Tell group members that it is more useful to allow the images to emerge and not try to change or edit them in any way. There is no right or wrong way to image. Also tell group members that they may deviate from the directions if that is what emerges for them. For example, when I participated in one imagery experience, the directions had me walking along a country road. In my imagery, I was walking along and there was a black and white cat like my cat on the side of the road. However, the facilitator gave a cue to image a cow. I chose to stick with the cat. After all, he was cow colored.

Group members should be made aware that they can stop the imaging at any time by opening their eyes. Since the leader cannot know what will emerge that is sensitive or significant for an individual, complete safety from unpleasant material cannot be guaranteed. Empower members to take care of their own safety by letting them determine when and whether to continue with imagery.

Follow steps described in the next section, Techniques for Structuring Guided Imagery.

After the guided imagery have participants draw, write or talk about what they experienced. If writing or drawing is selected as the response mode, materials should be readily available so that members move directly from imaging to drawing or writing. Care should be taken by the leader and members not to interpret their production. It is important to be accepting and non-judgmental. What emerges may be very sensitive, emotionally laden material for that person. He/she is more likely to continue to work with it for deeper understandings if no evaluative comments are made.

The leader should not interpret for members. If they are puzzled about their product, help them understand by exploring associations, not by providing interpretations. A process for doing this is described more fully under the section, Understanding What Emerged.

## TECHNIQUES FOR STRUCTURING GUIDED IMAGERY

The steps described here have their fullest application for the narrative guided imagery, but are also applicable to all imagery interventions. It may be helpful to help members relax before beginning the exercise as that may help produce more vivid images. Relaxation is advised even for very short guided imagery exercises.

### Introduction

The guided imagery activity is introduced with descriptions of what will be done, how it will be done, and for what reasons. Sanction is given for a variety of responses as there are no right or wrong ways to participate.

### Climate setting

A quiet, comfortable environment is provided. Group members are encouraged to lie on the floor if appropriate, or to get as comfortable as they can in their chairs and close their eyes. Semidarkness encourages production. Relaxation and sensory-awareness techniques help participants to screen out external stimuli. Music often helps to create a peaceful, relaxed mood, but should only be used before beginning the guided imagery. Do not use background music during the exercise as it may be distracting for some members. Further, the music itself may stimulate specific moods and images that are not consistent with the cues for imaging provided by the leader.

### Guiding

The leader offers brief, concise cues and directions which may suggest visualizations, colors, sounds, textures, smells, or activities. Guidance is limited to cues only; responses or feelings are not suggested.

The leader may want to observe participants closely for body reactions, movement, and so on, during the exercise. The time focus for imaging is kept in the present: that is, use the present tense when presenting cues. For example,

"You are walking across a meadow," not "You were or will be walking across a meadow."

### Pacing

Timing and pacing are critical in guided imagery. Allowing too little time truncates the experience for members, while too much time may distract or blur the focus. Spontaneous imagery may take only a minute. Other triggered images can produce useful material in five minutes or less, while an extensive guided imagery may last twenty or thirty minutes. It is often helpful to give time cues: "In another minute, I will be asking you to leave this place and return to the room."

### Terminating

The leader "returns" the members to the group room by calling attention to the real, external situation, and giving step-by-step instructions for reentry. A common termination goes as follows: "In a minute, I want you to return to this room. Begin stretching your arms and legs and, with your eyes remaining closed and at your own pace, slowly bring yourself to a sitting position. When you feel ready, slowly open your eyes."

### Sharing

Sharing of the imagery experience is an important final step. Individual group members can first take some time alone reflecting on the experience, then dyads or triads can be formed for interpersonal sharing. As a final step, sharing can continue in the large group. Guided imagery can be an intensely private experience; sanction should be given for sharing only what the member wants to share. However, some form of sharing is useful because it helps give closure.

## CONSIDERATIONS FOR USE

Use of guided imagery interventions should be influenced by several considerations prior to initiating the exercise: goals, voluntary participation, privacy, intensive and deep feelings aroused, associations, impact on the group and the level of trust.

### Goals

The purpose of using an imagery intervention should be clear to the leader and to group members.

### Voluntariness and Privacy

Group members should participate in guided imagery activities voluntarily. Some members may be fearful of imagery or believe that they are unable to image. Some members may want to keep their productions private. Sanction should be given for nonparticipation, and for the privacy of the experience.

### Depth and Heightened Affect

Guided imagery frequently serves to develop awareness of difficult issues and suppressed feelings. Care should be taken to offer group members support and security. The leader will need to prepare for expressions of joy, euphoria, sadness, and other emotions. Tears occasionally accompany a moving experience.

### Interpretation

Guided imagery productions have meaning primarily for the member who allowed the image to emerge. The leader may prompt group members to explore or to make associations to ambiguous parts of images for each other, but effort by the facilitator or other group members to interpret for others should be resisted. Leaders should be prepared to block evaluations or interpretations put forth by group members for images shared by other members. The focus should remain on personal associations by gruop members.

### Impact on the Group

Engaging in a guided imagery with a group has different effects: for some members, imagining is enhanced; for others, it is suppressed. Adequate processing of the experience requires sensitivity of the leader, especially when working with a member who is having difficulty understanding or accepting what emerged.

### Trust level

Guided imageries, in particular, require that some degree of trust be present before they are introduced. It is rarely wise to begin a group with an elaborate guided imagery activity.

## UNDERSTANDING WHAT EMERGED

A guided imagery experience can be very pleasant and enjoyable. Group members relax, become energized, and reflect on pleasing events, situations, people, or objects. However, if full therapeutic use is desired, then understanding of the material that emerged during imaging is necessary.

Emphasis when processing the experience is placed on the individual's making personal associations, not the counselor or other group members. Material and personal associations are more easily accepted if the individual makes the connections.

Begin the process of understanding what emerged with making arrangements for recording the experience. Recording can be via drawing, writing, or other means. Adults can usually retain enough of the experience to talk about it without first writing or drawing, but children and adolescents, as well as those adults with diminished cognitive and/or emotional capacities, will usually have difficulty doing so. However, even sophisticated adults will enjoy drawing what emerged, and some like to have a written record for reference.

### Using Drawings

Provide enough materials for each participant prior to initiating the guided imagery. After termination of imagery ask participants to draw what emerged. Each participant should have time to present his or her drawings in the session. Ask that members focus on what was significant for them during the experience and what the associations are for these significant points in their current life. Further areas for exploration are new understandings, options that emerged that were not previously in awareness, decisions made, or new awarenesses about self, others, and/or relationships. It is very important for each member to be able to present in the session. Avoid carrying over to the next session because the impact and immediacy will be lost. Leaders should plan so that there is sufficient time for all to present.

### Using Writing

After termination of guided imagery ask participants to write a description of the experience including as many details as possible and feelings or emotions experienced. Give an opportunity for each to report orally on as much or as little as he/she chooses. After this step, have participants focus on personal associations for significants in the imagery experience. These are written and can be explored more fully by either writing more about the associations or talking about them.

### When Group Member Is Stuck

Some images are difficult for individuals, usually because of resistance. It is not wise to address the resistance directly as it is there to protect the individual. If resistance is very strong, the best course may be to tell the person that this image seems important to him or her (after all, he/she selected it), and that since the association is not clear at this time, he/she may wish to continue considering its associations. Give permission to drop it for now and to work on it independently. Do not term it resistance or allow other members to do so. If the member him or herself terms it resistance, point out that it is there for a purpose and can be worked through at subsequent group sessions.

### Deepening the Experience

However, some resistances may be minimal and material can be accessed through the following process: concentrate on the image, reexperience feelings and emotions, allow meanings to emerge, concentrate on details and actions, dialogue with the images (Ahnsen 1977, p. 117). A brief description follows.

The therapist guides the group member through the process. Tell him or her that the process can be stopped at any time or when understanding is achieved by saying, Stop. Ask first that he/she concentrate on the image, focusing on a part that is significant and understood by him or her. Then ask the person to move to the part of the image that is puzzling. Allow time for movement. When he/she has arrived and can visualize or otherwise identify the puzzling part of the image, ask him or her to reexperience feelings (sensations) and emotions associated with the image and verbalize them out loud. The leader may need to write notes of the member's verbalizations, but not comment or explore at this time. Ask whether any meanings come to mind and remind him or her not to edit or change: just let them arise spontaneously.

If the process to this point has not produced new understandings or associations, ask that the person concentrate on details and describe them as fully as possible. Ask for more descriptives such as color, height, weight, or position. The final step is to have him or her dialogue with the image. Dialoguing means that the person says whatever he/she wishes to the image, verbalizes what the image replies, and continues doing so until the dialogue ceases of its own accord.

While the leader will not interpret for the member, he/she may decide to report the feelings experienced as the member worked through the process. For example, the leader may have felt a profound sense of sadness when the member described feelings and emotions associated with the image, and this sadness is what could be reported to the member.

This process is easily taught and learned. Group members can be encouraged to continue to use it on their own and may gain better connections to their inner and outer worlds through imagining and associating.

## SOME EXAMPLES OF GUIDED IMAGERY

The following imagery exercises are derived from the literature. The assumptions underlying each are that the cues evoke a universal response and that the images tap into continuing issues. Assagioli's symbols seem to be similar to those used in fairy tales and mythology that speak to continuing developmental issues.

Desoille (1966) used basic scenes on which he elaborated as he guided by providing cues. The following are some of the scenes: "Imagine descending into the depths of the ocean"; "Imagine entering a cave and finding a witch or wizard"; "Imagine entering a cave and finding a dragon."

Leuner (1969) starts each imagery with asking that you imagine yourself in a meadow. He then chooses one of nine options for the rest of experience.

1. Look for a pathway in the meadow, follow it to a forest at the foothills of a mountain, go through the forest. climb the mountain, and describe the view from the top. (This is said to represent the subject's pattern of aspiration, mastery, and achievement.)

2. Follow a brook upstream to its source or down to the ocean. (This represents the flow of psychic energy and the potential for emotional development.)

3. Explore a house.

4. Visualize a close relative.

5. Imagine a situation that is intended to evoke sexual feelings. For example (for a woman), imagine that your car has broken down and a driver offers you a lift. Or (for a man) see a rosebush, pick one of the roses, take it home, and put it in a vase on your desk.

6. Visualize a lion.

7. Say the name of a person of your own sex, then visualize a person who has this name.

8. Look into a dark forest or a cave.

9. See a swamp with a figure rising out of it.

Assagioli (1965) divides guided imagery symbols into seven categories. The goal for the imagery exercise determines the choice of symbols to include in the narrative.

1. Nature symbols, including mountains, the sea, rivers, lakes, wind, clouds, rain, fog, caves, trees, fire, plants (especially flowers), jewels, and the sun (which is an important symbol to psychosynthesis practitioners).

2. Animal symbols, both wild and domestic.

3. Human symbols: parents and other relatives, a wise person, magician, royalty, parts of the body (e.g., the heart), and such human processes as birth and death.

4. Constructed symbols such as bridges, channels, reservoirs, tunnels, roads, paths, walls, doors, houses, stairways, boxes.

5. Religious and mythological symbols: Christian, Eastern, pagan.

6. Abstract symbols: numbers, geometrical symbols of both two and three dimensions.

7. Spontaneous symbols emerging in dreams or daydreams, a category that cuts across the previous six.

Another psychosynthesis imagery exercise consists of asking the subject to visualize an image in response to each of the following questions:

1. Where are you right now in your life?

2. Where are you going?

3. What obstacles or barriers are in your way?

4. What qualities or things are needed to achieve your goal?

5. What will your life be like once your goal is reached?

Still another approach consists of asking the subject to visualize a door upon which appears a word suggested by the subject or the guide (e.g., fear, worry, hope, love). The subject is then asked to open the door. The door may be set in a wall, or it may be a door in a house, or it may be a door at the top or bottom of a stairway.

# 9

# DREAMS

## DEFINITIONS

### Similarities of Imagery and Dreams

There are several similarities between guided imagery and dreaming. They both bypass defenses, connect people to the deeper processes in their lives, and can promote healing. On the other hand, imagery may be less threatening because it is more under the individual's control as he/she can stop the process at any time by simply opening his or her eyes, whereas dreaming does not seem to be under conscious control.

Throughout the centuries, humans have felt that their dreams were significant. For example, some perceived dreams as messages from the gods or God, others saw dreams as attempts by demons to take control, others felt that dreams foretold the future, and still others felt dreams were communication with the dead. Freud, the father of psychology, gave dreams another definition: that of the royal road to the unconscious.

### Freud

Freud viewed fantasy and dreams as primary process events generated by the *id,* which he saw as the repository of primitive wishes, desires, and creativity. According to Freud, the id was repressed by the *ego*, that part of the personality that was logical and rational. He used free association and dream analysis to gain access to the unconscious. Freud felt that fantasies and dreams required interpretation since they were symbolic representations of hidden wishes and desires. The *projection hypothesis* proposes that we unconsciously externalize our wishes, desires, fears, and goals through projection. This concept receives support, not only from the psychoanalysts, but also from gestalt psychologists, whose studies provided evidence that internal needs of the individual are indirectly, and often ambiguously, reflected in fantasy life.

### Jung

To Freud, the unconscious was the repository of repressed wishes and memories, but to Jung it was a source of deep inner wisdom which, if contacted, might complement the wisdom of conscious life. For example, if conscious tendencies had been carried to extremes in certain directions, with other possibilities being ignored, images and symbols might show through the dream those tendencies that were being neglected and encourage their development.

Dreams, Jung wrote (1956, p. 141), "are nothing less than self-portraits of the psychic life-process." He went on to propose that dreams reveal the "real" state of the individual and are truthful. Because the individual represses, suppresses, or denies the "real" state of affairs, it impacts his or her life through symptoms. As long as the focus is on treating symptoms, not much therapeutic change takes place. Thus, it is important to understand dreams in order to identify the "real" problem so that an effective intervention can be made.

## EXAMPLES OF DREAM INTERPRETATIONS

### Methods of Understanding Dreams

Freud sought to interpret dreams for the patient (client). He felt that the therapist was the expert and understood the language of dreams. Dream analysis was primarily the therapist's telling the patient (client) what his or her dream meant.

Jung's introduction of noninterpretative methods was a striking innovation, the importance of which cannot be exaggerated. He warned against interpretation in some cases (1956, p. 225), recommending instead that one must come to a "settlement" with the unconscious by experiencing the "fantasies."

In order to experience fantasies, they must be directly confronted. If the image expresses itself in a voice, writes Jung (1960, p. 186), "it is technically very simple to note down the 'other' voice in writing and to answer its statements from the standpoint of the ego. It is exactly as if a dialogue were taking place."

Many have studied dreams and dreaming, trying to understand what meanings or messages are contained therein. Following is a literature review that describes some methods for analyzing dreams together with suggestions for use in group work.

### Daseinanalysis or Phenomenological Dream Interpretation

Condrau (1991) describes a process for analyzing dreams that considers the dream to be a part of immediate manifestation of life. This viewpoint asserts that dreams do *not* stand for something else. For example, dreams are not metaphors, re not mirroring the unconscious, or do not pursue a purpose. He writes that:

Daseinanalysis has a very simple frame of reference for interpreting dreams, namely, the three part question: Where is the dreamer in his (her) dream? Whom or what does he (she) meet? and, In what mood does he (she) experience the encounter?

This process involves telling the dream and answering the three-part question about the experience. The group leader would help the dreamer to clarify and expand the answers in order to derive as much understanding as possible. To use in group, have all members write a description of a dream and answer the questions. Processing could focus on what emerged for members as they reflected on their dream.

### Transpersonal Approach to Dream Analysis

Matos (1985) defines and describes a transpersonal approach to understanding dreams. *Transpersonal psychology* is defined as "the scientific study of states of consciousness" (p. 160), and it incorporates parts of other theories in psychology such as behaviorism, psychoanalysis, analytical psychology, and humanistic psychology.

Matos (1985) developed a technique he labels *day dream catharsis*. He uses it primarily with unfinished dreams, but it also appears to be a useful process for working with dream fragments.

The process begins with the dreamer lying on a couch, eyes closed, and relaxed. He/she is asked to recapture the feeling of the dream and retell the dream using the present tense. When the dreamer gets to the point where he/she stopped remembering the dream, he/she is asked to let the imagination supply the remainder. Matos finds that most people are able to recapture the rest of the dream at this point. He says, "In this inner psychotherapeutic dream journey the person may move from psychodynamic to perinatal and transpersonal levels of consciousness" (p. 161).

This method seems to be more useful in working with one member at a time. However, a group adaptation could be to guide all members in focusing on a dream or dream fragment and letting imagination fill in the gaps.

### Person-Centered Dream Analysis

Barrineau (1991) proposes a model for dream work based on *person-centered principles of actualization*, the assertion that locus of control lies with the client, and the facilitating attitude of the counselor. This approach to dream work uses a process of uncovering meaning as the client presents it, and focusing on present experiencing. It is based on assumptions that dreams are symbols or metaphors for the "real" world of the dreamer, and that translation of the symbols or metaphors is done by the dreamer guided by the counselor. Two types of questioning are used by the counselor, clarification and exploratory. In *clarification* the counselor makes sure he/she understands what the dreamer is saying and means. *Exploratory* questions are those that expand or deepen translation of symbols or metaphors.

Other techniques include reflective, "idiosyncratic" (p. 97), and cumulative responses. *Reflective* responses mirror that which the dreamer expressed, *idiosyncratic* responses reflect the understanding and genuineness of the counselor, and *cumulative* responses link and summarize expressions of the dreamer.

Each of these techniques require the leader to be knowledgable enough to ask the questions that will deepen the experience and help clarify the symbols or metaphors to be associated with current functioning.

### Gestalt

Feder and Rondall (1980) describe a gestalt approach to working with dreams by comparing it to the psychoanalytic approach. The gestalt approach assumes that the dream is a statement about one's existence, that is, fragmented parts of self, whereas the psychoanalytic approach assumes that the characters, events, and objects in the dream symbolize something about the inner experiencing of the individual. The gestalt approach uses the present tense when retelling the dream rather than the past or "talking about" the dream. The gestalt approach also assumes that "each person, event, or aspect of a dream reflects or projects a part of the dreamer. The function of the dreamwork is to bring into awareness all these parts and ultimately to integrate them" (p. 22).

The process used in the gestalt approach begins as the dreamer tells the dream in the present tense. After telling the dream, the dreamer explores parts of the dream as projections of self by becoming that part and retelling the dream from the perspective of the part. By assuming the roles of the fragmented, projected parts of self, the dreamer begins to realize what the various parts are trying to say, and what the existential message is.

Although only one dreamer can be worked with, it is helpful to have all group members write or draw a dream. As the leader guides one member in understanding their projections, other members follow along and learn the process for understanding their own projections portrayed in their dreams.

### Dream Appreciation Group

Each member of a *dream appreciation group* takes a turn in presenting a dream to the group, which becomes the focus for the group session (Sarlin 1991). At the first session the group leader lectures on dreams and describes the process that will be used.

The process consists of the following:

1. One member presenting a dream in as much detail as possible.

2. Other feelings, emotions, and meanings for the dream are suggested or reported by group members.

3. The dreamer responds to the remarks, reconstructs the emotional atmosphere of the day and thoughts before going to sleep.

4. A dialogue and replay of the dream, scene by scene, are presented with group members offering projective interpretations, reacting empathically or, listening.

5. At the next session, the dream is reviewed for any new thoughts, feelings, etc. before introducing the new dream.

### Dream Understanding Exercise

The *dream understanding exercise* process could be used in either individual or group counseling (Baylor and Deslauriers 1987). It provides a mechanism for each member to work on personal material and can be modified to provide for group interaction. There are five steps: recording, analyzing content, combining the dream and waking life script, problem-solving at the cast-specific level, and problem-solving at the organismic level. The process begins with writing a dream report, that is, as much information about the dream as possible.

1. Write a dream report. Afterward members are asked to note:
   a. associations for primary images,
   b. sketches--physical layouts of scenes,
   c. further associations, and
   d. a title for the dream.

2. Analyze content by selecting elements that express the essence of the dream and draw inferences. Look for repeating themes or ideas. Pay special attention to *metaphoric referents*: the symbols, characters, actions.

3. Relate the dream to the waking script.
   a. List four to five major episodes in the dream.
   b. Identify how the episodes follow one's life or life script. This becomes the waking life script.

4. Problem-solving at the cast-specific level.
   a. Note all deviations from the waking script (item 3).
   b. Describe the physical state (action) desired state, degree of attainment and possibilities.

5. Assessment and problem solving.

This method of understanding dreams is very time consuming and may be more appropriate for a group that uses dream interpretation as a major technique.

### Dream Mapping

The *dream mapping* process (Morrison 1990) describes dream analyses for individuals in recovery. While they are characteristic dreams for individuals who abused alcohol, the process can be adapted for other conditions where members are trying to make behavioral changes in their lives and there is fear that they will be drawn back into the undesired state or behavior.

Dreams about recovery have the following patterns:

Stage 1 "The Dark Night": dreams are described as full of dread and terror. There are dreams of destruction, death, guilt, and persecution. These usually occur before treatment.

Stage 2 "Pandora's Box": Dreams have themes of alienation, violence, mutilation, bizarre sexuality and persecution. (First stage of recovery)

Stage 3 "The Dragon Fight": Confrontation and battle are the themes. Dreams are of struggle for control of self, such as battles with demons, over ownership and assumption of the role of hero(ine).

Stage 4 "Rebirth": Dreams describe new living spaces, positive movement, acceptance, spiritual presence, rescue, ownership, and positive identification.

Stage 5 "The Descent": Dreams place the dreamer in situations involving cognitive dissonance and guilt (temporary relapse, or "dry drunk").

Stage 6 "The Return": The dreams go back to much of what occurs in stage 4.

### Dream Oriented Group

The *dream analysis* process is used in a dream-oriented group where members meet to work on meanings in personal dreams (Shuttleworth, et al. 1988). As this method leads to rapid revealing of unconscious material, it is not suitable for clients who are psychotic or prepsychotic. Further, the group leader needs to have preparation in depth psychology as well as experience in leading groups.

Members decide when they wish to explore a dream and can terminate the process at any stage. Other group members present ideas and make suggestions about the dream, but control remains with the presenter. The group begins with an introduction to the process, theoretical foundations, and rules governing participation.

Following is the process used in analyzing dreams.

1. Group members participate in relaxation exercises to encourage and promote imagery.

2. The dreamer presents a statement of dream content, reinvoking imagery, details, and other aspects of the dream. No interpretations or associations are given in this stage.

3. In amplification the dreamer identifies links between the dream and his or her waking life. Hypotheses are offered by group members and the leader on the dream images.

4. All members and the leader participate in helping the dreamer isolate theme(s), and identify problems that emerged through amplification.

5. Interpretation and validation of the dream are accomplished through
   a. commentary on the predominant mood of the dream, and
   b. a time perspective, relating the dream to past, present, and future possibilities.

6. Termination

Interpretation in step 5 uses Jung's four sequential phases: *exposition*--a statement of setting, characters, and state of the dreamer; *plot development*; *culmination*--a dramatic change or shift in the dream or a significant event; and *lysis*--the result or solution desired by the dreamer (Jung, 1958).

## Prolucid Semantics Technique

Ahnsen's (1988) method of dream analysis, the *prolucid semantics techniques*, parallels his process for imagery with the focus of interpretation on associations with mother and father.

The process would be appropriate in a group setting and would allow individuals to work on personal dreams. It begins with having the member(s) retell the dream. If it is used in a group, each member could write a description of the dream. The rest of the process follows.

1. Members are asked to select a word from the dream after retelling the dream.

2. After choosing a word, they identify what the word means to them.

3. The leader instructs them to "keep your mother in mind, look at the word and meaning, and describe in detail what it means."

4. When associations with the mother are complete, the leader instructs them to do the same thing, keeping father in mind.

5. The process can be used for additional words for more clarification.

## Dream Enlargements

Progoff's approach (1977), to understanding dream material, that of *dream enlargements*, assumes that dreams contain material that is important on many levels. Dreams reflect the objective circumstances, current problems and fears, and hopes and goals. On the other level, they also reflect deeper goals that are emerging and are not yet in awareness: deeper goals such as long-range purposes that set the fundamental directives of a life. Sometimes there are destructive patterns and purposes in one's life of which he/she is not aware, but have a negative impact in their relation to other life goals. Dreams can bring these goals, purposes, and patterns to the fore. Dreams can also reflect tensions and anxieties that arise out of conflict between immediate desire and requirements of long-range goals. Many of these conflicts are not conscious. Dreams express them, and carry them further toward resolution. While the difficulties regarding the personal contents of life are being resolved, the dream movement is making one aware of unrealized *potentials* of his or her life.

The process begins with keeping a dream log over a period of time. Series of dreams tend to produce more material than does a single dream. Recordings in the log should contain as much detail as possible, and when entire dreams are not remembered, fragments should be recorded.

The dream log only records dreams and gradually a moving picture of the continuity of dream life is accumulated. Group members are asked not to try to analyze or interpret, just record. When reading back over the dreams, they are instructed to try to reenter the movement of the dream process as a whole.

The first step is to read over the dream log and deliberately refrain from analyzing content.

The second step is to return to the place, time, and so on, where the dreaming occurred and try to reenter the dreams. The dreamer is instructed to place him or herself in the flow of imagery and not consciously select a dream, but let the selection be spontaneous.

The third step is to let the atmosphere of the dream establish itself again. Once the atmosphere is established, reread the few dreams preceding the one selected and the few that come after. The idea is to experience the *series* of dreams. If the dream selected emerges as significant but is not recorded in the dream log, record it at that point.

The dreamer is instructed to reenter the series of dreams and let them flow: to allow the images, feelings, and actions to happen, and not try to direct or analyze.

Step four begins after reentering and reexperiencing. The dreamer is instructed to record these feelings, images, and so forth. The feelings, images, and so on, may be in bits and pieces and may not form an understandable whole at this point.

After recording, the dreamer rereads the continuation of the dreaming and records the feelings and emotions that took place then, and are taking place now.

Processing of dream material is structured by the leader. The following questions form the focus and responses are recorded.

While these experiences were taking place, what feelings were present? What was the atmosphere?

Do you perceive a direction within it?

Do you feel a particular theme or message?

Was the message or direction present in the reentry of dreaming, or do you perceive it now?

Are there new thoughts, intuitions, or recognitions spontaneously welling up? Record them.

Reread them.

The leader then asks members to go back to the original sequence of dreams and feel the emotional tone and movement. Add to this the experiences of the reentry and draw the two together and feel them as one. When this experience is full, stop the movement. Hold it. Now, reflect on your outer life's sequence during this period. Feel the rhythm, flow, change--the combination of circumstances that carry into the recent period. Feel everything of life: hopes, fears, people, inner and outer events.

Visualize the outer life sequence on one side and the dream experience and symbols on the other side. On one side is the conscious life and on the other is the unified movement of inner nonconscious life. Balance one against the other. Let the two sides equalize.

What do these two sides of life have to say to each other? What do they say to you when you see them side by side? Record this.

After completing this sequence the group leader can focus processing on having members report what emerged as an understanding of their dream. Links to relationships and events in and out of group can be described, particularly when linkages can be made between members' dreams that relate to the group

## OTHER METHODS OF DREAM INTERPRETATION

### Symbols as Metaphors and Analysis

The use of symbols as metaphors is another method that involves writing and lends itself to use in a group. After each member completes the process on his or her personal dream, it is helpful for him or her to share the analyses or outcome in the group.

1. Write the dream, using the present tense. Include as much detail as possible: characters, actions, feelings, sounds, colors, smells, and so on.

2. Read the entire dream and underline seven to ten words. Short phrases can also be used but try to avoid whole sentences.

3. Members are instructed to make two to three significant statements about themselves and/or their life for each underlined word. Try to associate the underlined word with feelings, people, circumstances, events, and, most of all, how one sees him or herself.

4. Read the sentences and try to link them to self and waking life. Then write a paragraph about the themes, issues, concerns, or part of life revealed in the sentences.

5. Reread what you have written to this point and give your dream three titles.

6. Select one title and write a brief paragraph about yourself on the theme of the title.

### Cinquain

A *cinquain* (pronounced sin-cain) can transform dream symbols so that the meaning becomes more apparent. It is five lines graduating from a one- or two-syllable word or words, to four or eight syllables, and decreasing back to one or two syllables. A single cinquain uses the format 1, 2, 4, 2, 1; a double cinquain uses the form 2, 4, 8, 4, 2.

1. Line 1 names the image.

2. Line 2 describes the image.

3. Line 3 tells its use.

4. Line 4 tells how you feel about it.

5. Line 5 renames the image.

An example of a cinquain is:

House (names the image)
Cluttered (describes the image)
Shelter, comfort (tells the image's use)
Secure (tells how you feel about the image)
Vistas (renames the image)

Once the image is renamed and feelings about it are clearer, the meaning of the image is generally better understood. For example, in the preceding cinquain, the image could be interpreted as providing so much security that vistas are limited or constrained. The group member provides the meaning.

When using a cinquain in group:

1. Begin by having a member select two to three significants from his or her dream. The images may be persons, places, objects or actions.

2. Each member chooses an image and writes a cinquain.

3. Reflect on the renamed image and see whether it provides new understandings.

4. Repeat the process for the other selected images.

5. Link renamed images to determine symbolic representation or message.

### Draw A Dream

This exercise can highlight similarities between group members, and/or reduce anxieties members may have about being weird or different. Having others tell a story that is accurate in many respects about their dream from the drawing they produced helps members recognize similarities.

Group members are provided paper and colored markers and asked to recall a dream and draw a scene from the dream that conveys the essence of the dream. The dream can be a current one, a recurring dream, or one that they had some time ago.

After drawings are complete, all are put into the middle of the table or floor. Each member selects a drawing, not his or her own. Taking turns, each tells a story about the drawing he/she has selected. The leader takes care to ensure that stories about the drawing are not interpretations and that other group members do not interpret. If members seem to have difficulty telling a story, the leader can guide the process by having them describe what they see in the picture and imagine what happened before the picture and what the characters will do after this scene.

In the next step group members take back their drawings and report the accuracies, possibilities, and so forth, present in the story told by someone else.

### Image Expansion

*Image expansion* is a useful process when an image or symbol continues to evade understanding by the dreamer. He/she remains puzzled. While it may be tempting to interpret for the person, the material is more likely to be accepted if he/she produces the meaning. The process of expanding the image or symbol can produce additional meanings.

This is also a useful process that all members can participate in to expand the understanding of images and symbols that appear to be understandable. It is possible that there are levels of meanings to many images and symbols.

1. Draw an image from the dream.

2. Reflect on the image and consider its associations.

3. Add splashes of colors around the image that portray the feelings and emotions associated with the image--not just the feelings and emotions that are related to the dream.

4. Add drawings of people, actions, and other items associated with the image in waking life.

5. Review what has been done and report on any new awarenesses or understandings that emerged.

### Nightmares

Nightmares are dreams too. Mack (1970) defines a *nightmare* as "an anxiety dream in which fear is of such intense degree as to be experienced as overwhelming by the dreamer and to force partial awakening" (p. 2). Nightmares have three basic features: a sense of danger and helplessness; overwhelming anxiety, which may be experienced as dread, fright, or terror; and the threat of or actual attack on the dreamer as a character in the dream.

Mack (1970) proposes that nightmares contain and are representative of early, profound anxieties and conflicts experienced by all humans: anxieties and conflicts such as those around destructive aggression, separation, abandonment, loss of identity, devouring or being devoured, and fusion with mother. These internal and basic anxieties and conflicts threaten the survival of the ego and are likely to be associated with external threats to the individual. These external threats may not be in the individuals awareness, but exist on the unconscious or preconscious level, emerging in the nightmare in the guise of transformed symbols. The external danger taps underlying basic anxieties and conflicts around early issues that continue to impact the individual.

Nightmares appear to arise when the individual is facing a life circumstance that has traumatic implications for him or her, such as job loss, death, or other changes in the person's life. Sometimes, nightmares occur after a traumatic event. Another trigger for nightmares are conflicts children, adolescents, and adults have around completion of a developmental task. The state of interpersonal relationships with significant others in their life may produce nightmares. Another category of conditions that contribute to having a nightmare are physiological conditions, such as alcohol abuse and recovery, reactions to medication, and recovery from anesthesia.

Nightmares contain such material about the individual's perception of his or her inner and external world. They, too, can be analyzed and used as mechanisms for helping individuals to become aware of basic issues and conflicts arising from early experiences, and the relationship of these to current experiencing and/or functioning.

# 10

# WRITING

## READING AND WRITING AS EXPRESSIVE PROCESSES

### Description

Reading and writing can also be forms of expressive processes in group counseling. Whilc one does not create a product using reading as a process, directed or focused reading can stimulate creativity, promote realizations of commonalities, suggest possibilities and untapped potentials, give reasons for hope to flourish, provide information and guidance, and help develop conscious awareness of existential concerns.

Writing as an expressive process is more direct than reading, particularly when the individual taps into inner experiencing and is encouraged to explore and express that which emerges in written words. Some group members may be more adept in using written expression than others, but there are activities that almost all can use effectively, even members with relatively scant verbal skills. Directed or focused writing has the same possibilities as does focused or directed reading, and has an additional potential to create a product. Further, writing activities have an advantage over other forms of expressive processes such as art or imagery, in that writing can be a broader or more elaborate experience for the group member. It can encompass more details and in-depth exploration, and, as with other forms such as art, there can be a permanent record.

## READING AS AN EXPRESSIVE PROCESS IN GROUP

Bibliotherapy has long been recognized and accepted as a valuable activity. Many books are available for almost all reading levels featuring or focusing on a particular condition or situation such as terminal illness, death, or divorce. These books on specific conditions, or situations, often provide a list of readings on the subject that are recommended as useful for someone undergoing the condition or situation. Finding suitable materials does not appear to be difficult.

What is more difficult is using them effectively in group counseling. It is easier to see how to use guided reading with individuals, even with individuals in a group, but it is more difficult to use guided reading for the group.

Theme groups, such as those for divorce, death, cancer, alcoholism, can find and use readings more easily than groups without a specific clear theme, such as personal growth groups. However, even within the theme groups there are varying levels and needs of group members. Even though conditions and situations may be similar for members, they will respond very differently to the same reading material. Some may derive a lot of benefit, while others may not perceive any reference at all to their specific situation.

### Selection of Materials

Before introducing reading into the group the leader should have a very good understanding of the reading level of each member, and an awareness of a primary issue or need for each member, such as dependency. Understanding a primary issue or need allows the leader to select materials that also relate to this issue and, thereby, provide the individual with material that is appealing, leading to a greater likelihood of use and internalization. For example, if a group has been formed for children of divorced parents and the leader chooses reading material that focuses on having dependency needs met although members', or many members', primary needs at this point focus on safety or an existential need of fear of the unknown, the group is unlikely to understand or accept that the reading material has relevance for them.

*Reading Level.* Material selected for reading should be on a level that is easily understood by group members. The purpose is to inform and teach about the situation, conditions, possibilities, unrealized potentials, and so on, but not to teach reading. Most group members are more apt to stick with reading if it is well within their ability to understand. It is probably better to have reading material at a relatively lower level than at a too complex level.

*Degree of Abstractness/Complexity.* Some points to consider when choosing material are the degree of abstractness, complexity of ideas presented, vocabulary, and length. Highly educated and/or intellectual group members may be comfortable with very abstract material. Some may enjoy the challenge of following an abstraction in its many possibilities, potentials, and manifestations. Members who are more concrete and practical may become impatient at the ambiguous nature of abstractions and derive little or no benefit. Other group members may be so mired in their misery that they cannot concentrate on or follow abstract material.

Most conditions, situations, problems, or issues of group members are complex. However, reading material should not be selected to further a focus on complexity to the extent that it confuses rather than informs. It is very useful for members to recognize the complexity because it prevents them from expecting quick and simple answers or solutions. It is not beneficial for them to become even more confused as confusion may lead to feelings of hopelessness or helplessness. Material selected should help to clear up some confusion, not increase it.

*Jargon Free.* Material used in focused directed reading should be free of jargon and other words that are not usually used. If the group is built around a shared medical condition it may be difficult to present information that is jargon-free. However, every effort should be made to select material that does not force the reader to a dictionary or other sources in order to understand. While learning new words or looking up meanings in the dictionary is commendable and something to be encouraged, having to do so may discourage some members from reading the material, and the expected benefits will be lost. Further, jargon cannot be found in a dictionary unless it is a specialized dictionary, such as one for medical terms.

*Length.* Length is also a consideration. Some members may read very rapidly, so that length is not a problem for them. Others may read slowly and more deliberately, and length may present them with a problem. Long, involved, complex, and/or abstract material may appear overwhelming and not worth the effort. Further, how many sessions over what period is the group scheduled to meet? Reading material should have the capability of being completed before the group is completed if it is to be a part of group process. Adjunct reading material that is informative and can be left to the individual's choice is being not considered in this discussion on bibliotherapy. When reading is optional and the leader does not intend to use it in the group, length does not become a concern. If reading is planned as part of the group process, then length is an issue just as complexity, level of reading ability required, and abstractness are of concern. The leader will want to select material that may be too succinct, that is, short, and trust that members who want more will seek it out on their own.

*Collecting Materials.* Group leaders are encouraged to collect and have available a variety of reading materials that can be used as bibliotherapy in groups. Collect materials that are factual about conditions of group members, for example books and pamphlets on eating disorders. Also helpful are biographies and autobiographies of individuals who have experienced similar situations or conditions, fiction that presents issues and/or themes similar to those of group members, self-help books and materials that are written by recognized experts in the field, cartoons and other humorous materials, and articles from professional journals around a particular topic. For the more educated or interested group member, a list of references could be useful.

The group leader may also wish to find out which libraries in the immediate area have the reading material. Members *can* also be referred to this source.

*Advantages.* Using reading materials in the group can enhance process by clarifying information about a condition or topic, showing that there is hope, and presenting possibilities for change. Group members may have misinformation or misperceptions about a condition. Instead of using group time to clear up this confusion, readings can be assigned and a part of a session used to make sure members all understood the information and implications.

Reading about someone who had a similar condition, problem or issue and was able to overcome, adjust to, or function in spite of it may be helpful to some group members. Realizing that the situation or condition need not be hopeless can inspire them to feel that they too can get better. Unless members feel hopeful they are unlikely to be active participants in their own counseling. Hope can be an encouragement to persevering and action.

Many times group members are so close to their problems, or mired in misery, or overwhelmed by despair that they fail to see possibilities that can lead to positive changes and outcomes. Reading about others in similar situations and what actions they took can help some members begin to generate possibilities for themselves. The idea behind bibliotherapy is not that they do what the real or fictional character did in the book, but that they realize that one can get out of the misery and/or despair and generate ideas of how that can be accomplished.

## WRITING AS AN EXPRESSIVE PROCESS IN GROUP

### Advantages

Guided writing has several advantages: it allows for personal expression, it can maintain privacy and confidentiality, it can be used to guide and focus introspection, and it can provide a record of thoughts, ideas, feelings, and emotions. The activity chosen can broaden and deepen self-exploration, be a means for clarification, express ambiguous or complex feelings and emotions, or intensify and narrowly focus on an important piece of personal material. Use of writing in the group permits all members to work on their issues at the same time.

### Disadvantages

There are also disadvantages. Resistance can be maintained, especially if the written material is not shared or disclosed to the group in any way. The other group members and leader can provide reality checks that strip away rationalizations and self-deceptions when material is shared in the group. Another disadvantage can be the need for consistent writing over a period, such as when diaries or journals are used. Some members may have difficulty sticking to the task and thereby lose much of the intended effectiveness of the activity. Members' verbal skills and comfort with writing may also present difficulties if either, or both, are low. Writing cannot be used effectively if there is considerable resistance to the activity.

Another major disadvantage of writing activities is the limited application to group and group process. The personal nature of writing and the degree to which it can be private and confidential mean that the group need not be involved. Writing activities can be very useful for individuals but less so for the group.

### Examples of Writing as an Expressive Process

There are several forms of writing that lend themselves to use in group work: journals, poetry, autobiographies, dialogues, letters, and stimulus pieces. Each of these will be described with applications to individuals and group process. Because writing can be personal and private, it is relatively nonthreatening for most group members and can be used at every stage of group development.

### Journals and Diaries

Journals and diaries are ways of providing chronological records of events. The tendency of many who write journals or diaries is to record facts. Guided journal and diary writing provides a framework for what experiences and emotions are to be focused on and recorded. For example, a daily diary should record more than events. The range of emotions experienced, high points, low points, significant ideas and thoughts, dreams of the night before, musings about relationships or possibilities add to the factual record and provide a more balanced and comprehensive account for the individual. It can then help him or her to focus better on feeling and experiencing the richness or poverty in his or her life. An exercise that is useful has group members keeping a specific journal or diaries. The specific nature not only focuses their efforts but can help provide material to be used in the group. Examples of specific journals or diaries are a daily diary, a dream diary, a journal of events with elaborations, a journal recounting situations and events around relationships, a journal of feelings and emotions which elaborates and expands on experiencing. Group sessions would then allow opportunities for sharing and exploring awarenesses developed as a result of writing. The leader can teach members how to use these accounts in a way to extract new awarenesses and understandings of self, and not have them be just recording exercises. This is accomplished by having members focus on or emphasize feelings and emotions connected with the situation, event, idea, person, and so forth. These feelings and emotions carry significant information that can aid members gain better understanding of self, others, and the situation.

Feelings and emotions generated in writing journals and diaries also provide clues to associations with past events that may be significant, and/or link the past to present experiencing and relationships. Feelings and emotions experienced in relation to present events, situations, and persons are very often associated with others in the past, such as that which happens in transference. They may also represent, in part, projections and introjections. Guiding members to use feelings and emotions to determine past associations with current situations and relationships can be beneficial.

During the process of teaching members to use journals and diaries effectively the leader can show members how to recognize and extract hope from their writings. Pointing out possibilities, strengths, and unrealized potentials contributes to developing hopefulness. Individuals may be too close to the issue or problem to perceive solutions or resolutions. They may not realize what seeds of hope are already present, and other members and the leader can do much to point this out to them. The fact that the hope seen by others comes from what the individual has written, allows him or her to accept and capitalize on it.

Journals and diaries can also be the source for deriving creative energy. Recording feelings, thoughts, and concepts can lead to creative products such as poems, songs, and essays.

### Guided Life Exploration

Progoff (1977) used guided writing in a journal format. The writing occurred over two to three days, focused on recall of specific events, exploration of relationships, potentials, significants in different life situations; dialogues; and the physical, emotional, and spiritual dimensions of one's life. His book describes the process used in workshops and can easily be modified for group counseling.

The format I use regardless of time involved is to introduce the activity as a personal and private way of putting your life in focus. If it is a one-session workshop, group members are not introduced to each other and name tags are not used. Rules for participation are for each person to control the amount and event of his or her self-disclosure, to try not to edit, evaluate, or change material that emerges during the activity. When opportunities for reading aloud are provided, members are asked not to interpret or analyze, but to be accepting and nonjudgmental, and most importantly, to work on their own issues.

The Intensive Journal process used by Progoff takes at least three full days to complete when all sections are used. In addition, autobiographical data is compiled prior to the process--the Life History Log; in addition, a Daily Log is kept for a period of time, and a Dream Log is kept and/or compiled. The process can be adapted for a shorter period or completed over several sessions. I have found that a one-day session can produce much relevant material and members can be taught how to continue to explore on their own.

Major sections I adapted and always include are Becoming present-centered, Steppingstones, Intersections, working with a daily log and a dream log, and one or two dialogues.

*Becoming Present-Centered.* Focusing on the recent period in one's life helps members to become present-centered and to become more aware of where they are at this moment in their lives. It includes the recent past, and members may be just beginning a new period, in the middle of, or coming to the end of it.

*Steppingstones.* These are the significants in one's life throughout the stages beginning with birth. The list of events, situations, and people begins to define possible unfinished business, especially if intense affect is still associated with any "Steppingstone(s)." An opportunity is given to explore one or more in-depth at the workshop and members are encouraged to use the process for all items on the list.

*Intersections.* This section deals with experiences, choices, and decisions made by self and others that significantly influenced the direction one's life took.

Unrealized potentials and/or possibilities that were discarded or overlooked can reemerge and be considered. This section allows members to become more aware of the implications and impact these intersections had and are still having in their lives today. It also teaches members that they should consider alternatives fully before making decisions and choices, and that they do have some control over what happens to them.

*Daily Log*. Keeping a daily log that records feelings and emotions throughout the day, thought processes, quality of relationships, inner experiencing, the high point, and the low point helps the person to realize the dynamic quality of life. While specific events may be important, they do not define the entire experiencing. This log is more than simply a record of events. As members read their logs they become more aware of their total lives, opportunities presented, choices available, and potentials.

*Dream Log*. While one dream can produce considerable material with which to work, a series of dreams can better help identify issues, problems, and concerns. Members are asked to keep a dream log in which they record dreams and fragments of dreams. Even keeping a dream log for a week is very useful. Members are shown various ways of analyzing and understanding dreams. This is covered more fully in Chapter 9.

*Dialogues*. All of the dialogues are explorations and expansions of relationships: relationship with one's physical self, with significant events, with individuals who were and are important, with work or other projects considered important at various life stages, and with the cultural and societal forces that shaped the person. Each dialogue begins with recalling and reexperiencing the relationship during the period when it occurred. Feelings and emotions associated with the relationship are very important, and recall and reexperiencing are emphasized. Just because the relationship is in the past does not mean it is over, and this section provides an opportunity either to begin termination, reenergize the relationship, or resolve conflicting feelings and emotions.

*Working Format*. When using this adapted process in a workshop format I usually mail a description of the process in advance and ask participants to keep daily and dream logs and bring them to the workshop. I usually begin a one-day workshop with an art activity--drawing a life line with symbols for significant stages as events. This activity seems to help members begin the process of reflection. Throughout the day I make adjustments to the intended schedule, depending on participants' needs and time available. Members are given an opportunity to share in small groups what they have written after each session with no analysis, interpretation or evaluation by members or the leader.

### Poetry as a Reading and/or Writing Expressive Process

Poetry is an excellent way for some members to express complex thoughts, feelings, and/or emotions. Meaning can be conveyed through verse rather than prose. Members can write poems around their own personal experiences or how they experience other group members, or the leader can suggest specific topics or themes that lend themselves to this kind of expression. Topics or themes such as loneliness, feelings of abandonment or rejection, termination of a relationship, and love are examples.

Members can also be encouraged to read or can be assigned specific poems around a theme or issue. Sometimes others have expressed our feelings and emotions in their poetry. Reading how others express a similar emotion can promote awareness of universality and reduce feelings of alienation and isolation.

Poems written by members or others can be acted out in the session. Becoming the experience or emotion can help in understanding it and even with empathizing with others.

### Writing an Autobiography

Writing an autobiography can help accomplish several things. It can help individuals recall significant events, situations, and relationships with others in their lives; recall dimly remembered or forgotten material; stimulate recall of supplemental material associated with these important events, situations and/or relationships; reduce the need to storytell; and help focus on relevant material with which to work on in the group.

An autobiography can take several forms: an outline, a Book of Self, or an extensive written life history. Members who are not prone to get involved in writing an extensive life history can benefit from the other two activities.

*An Outline.* Members are directed to write an elaborate table of contents for an autobiography. Each chapter defines a particular chronological period and specific topics listed. For example, one chapter could be

Chapter Four--Senior in high school worried about college acceptance fell in love; was elected homecoming princess; snuck out without parents' permission; experienced the death of a grandmother; attended senior prom.

Processing of the activity would emphasize recall, reexperiencing, forgotten material, gaps, feelings, and emotions.

*Book of Self.* This is a homework activity that requires time to complete. Time must also be allowed for members to share if they wish.

The "Book of Self" begins with a brief biographical sketch. This is usually limited to one to three pages. Next come photographs of the person at various stages of life. Also included are pictures of other persons, pets, events, things, and so on. It should be noted that many members go to great lengths to secure photographs, even writing to relatives. Others go through their collections and have a pleasant time recalling past events and relationships. They may also become more aware of gaps in their lives or memories.

Awards, certificates, and other forms of appreciation and recognition form the next section. Hobbies and recreation activities can also be included in some way.

Depending on the educational level and age of group members, brief essays or poems on selected topics can be included. Topics such as grief, success, and loneliness, could be explored.

A summary statement or a collage of self as the person is today forms the final part.

### Written Dialogues

Written dialogues are a means to communicate with images, symbols, aspects of self, people, and/or events with whom there is unfinished business. The gestalt exercise of top dog-underdog (conflicting sides of oneself) is one example of an oral dialogue which can be very useful. However, written dialogues are an activity that several can engage in simultaneously, each one working on his or her personal issue(s).

A dialogue begins when the leader directs members to get in touch with an image, symbol, aspect of self, or a person and/or activity with whom there is unfinished business. Have members focus on the person or subject of the dialogue and allow the person's or subject's essence to emerge into awareness. It is very important that feelings and emotions associated with the person or subject be experienced, as they help the dialogue to unfold. Members are then directed to write a dialogue with the person or subject recording what they say or want to say to the person or subject, and what the responses are. The dialogue continues until it is finished.

Dialogues can be about relationships, conflicts, perceptions, expression of feelings and/or emotions, or any topic that is important for that member. Often the level and extent of the member's relationship with the person or subject become clearer as well as decisions made or to be made.

### Other Stimulus Materials for Writing

There are a variety of short writing activities that can be used to stimulate introspection and exploration of issues. Group leaders should remember that the purpose is to stimulate thoughts, feelings, and emotions, and choose an activity that focuses on a significant exploration of material for group members. Following are some examples.

*Being Remembered.* Members are directed to write a one page obituary. The obituary should have facts such as date of birth, employment, degrees, and so forth; current relationships that are important; and one way they wish to be remembered or something they did.

*Tombstone.* Members are presented with a sheet of paper with a tombstone on it. They are asked to fill it out with date of birth, their most relevant current relationship, and a short statement that captures the essence of their lives, their relationships, or that for which they wish to be remembered.

*Eulogy.* This activity is a longer version of Being Remembered and Tombstone. Members are asked to write a comprehensive eulogy that presents the essence of their lives from birth to the present. As this activity takes more thought and time to complete, members could do this as a homework activity. The leader could have each member read his or her own eulogy out loud or exchange eulogies and read someone else's.

*Letters.* A subject and topic are selected prior to beginning a letter. A subject is another person with whom the member wants to communicate or an aspect of self. Topics may be an exploration of the relationship, expressions of feelings and emotions, clarification of misunderstandings, and/or definition of a conflict. Members are encouraged to read the letter to the group.

# 11

# FAIRY TALES

## INTRODUCTION AND RATIONALE

### Use in Group Work

Fairy tales have the potential to be therapeutically useful for all age groups. They are not just for children, but can present adolescents and adults with an opportunity to become more aware of unresolved developmental and existential issues that continue to have significant impact on their current functioning.

### Work on Personal Issues

When fairy tales are used in a group setting they allow each member to work on personal issues within the group setting while also providing an opportunity to illustrate universality, instillation of hope, normal development, and common fears. Whether used on an individual or a group basis, fairy tales also suggest possibilities for resolution of conflicts and problems; give encouragement that one can "overcome": that is, you do not have to remain stuck, and you are capable and competent in the face of adversity and obstacles. Fairy tales allow individuals to externalize internal conflicts, and to integrate polarities.

### Awareness of Developmental Issues

Common metaphors and symbols in fairy tales recur and relate to experiences throughout one's life. They assume different meanings as circumstances and the self change, but continue to provide meanings and understandings. For example, the symbol of being lost in the forest can be understood as a metaphor for the search for meaning, direction, and/or understanding in one's life. A child can identify with it because he/she is constantly being faced with a world that is confusing and complex, and it is expected that they will "find their way" with proper guidance. The adolescent can also relate to the metaphor as he/she too is constantly being presented with options, choices, and the need to make life decisions, as well as trying to understand who he/she is and where he/she fits in. An adult, at almost any stage, can find meaning in the metaphor because of changing life circumstances, crises, and other events over which he/she may have little control.

## THEORETICAL FOUNDATIONS

The therapeutic use of fairy tales relies on assumptions embedded primarily in object relations, psychoanalytic, Jungian, and existential theories. Theories provide a basis for understanding what growth and development issues are addressed in fairy tales, and the implications of these issues in products of group members. Further, much of what is experienced in relation to fairy tales appears in symbolic or metaphoric form and personal associations must be made if they are to be understood. The process and understandings emerge from the theoretical perspective. Themes in fairy tales and group members' products speak of universal human struggles. While this is a continuing issue, different themes are important for an individual at different times in his or her life. Theory helps identification of the particular theme or themes.

### Object Relations and Psychoanalytic Theory

Both object relations and psychoanalytic theories have extensive emphases on early development, particularly on psychological development. Present day therapists operate on the assumption that much of the functioning and relationships later in life are a direct outcome of psychological development successes and failures, beginning with birth. A good and nurturing parental relationship is crucial for healthy development, and severe conditions, such as borderline and narcissistic disorders, can result if there are significant gaps or failures in early nurturing and/or psychological development. Fairy tales almost always deal with psychological development, with developmental tasks in childhood, and with relations with others, especially parents. They do much to point out that there are many commonalities among individuals in childhood experiences, such as sibling rivalry. Fairy tales, unlike myths, teach that ordinary individuals can endure, overcome, and succeed.

### Jungian Theory

Jungian or analytic psychology emphasizes the impact of early developmental issues on later functioning as they appear through metaphors and symbols. This theory proposes an underlying "collective unconscious" that is universal to all human beings. Thus, individuals have a personal unconscious that is uniquely theirs, and a universal one that is shared with all others in the world. Fairy tales present parts of the shared unconscious through the use of universal symbols, as well as having an overlay of symbols from the personal unconscious. There are elements of the individual's past, all of humankind's past and experiences, and present experiencing in responding to and understanding fairy tales. These all appear in fairy tales and individuals' respond to them as symbols and metaphors. Jungian psychology has contributed a great deal to the understanding and use of symbols and metaphors on both the personal and the universal level.

### Existential Theory

Existential themes of death, loneliness, alienation, and responsibility are present in fairy tales. These themes are perceived to be characteristic of the human condition, and to have an impact on past, present, and future functioning. These are the themes and issues with which all humans struggle, whether or not they are recognized as existential in nature. Fairy tales present existential themes and, by doing so, affirm the universality of the themes, and give hope that they can be dealt with effectively, even if they are not capable of resolution.

## EFFECTIVENESS OF FAIRY TALES

The following study demonstrates one approach to the efficacy of using a fairy tale to identify developmental and existential issues.

### A Study Using Fairy Tales with Adolescents and Adults

The purpose of this study (Brown 1993) was to determine whether developmental and existential issues could be identified through scenes selected by participants for drawing after hearing the fairy tale "Hansel and Gretel."

The Grimm brothers' version of "Hansel and Gretel" was used, and symbols identifying developmental and existential issues described by Bettelheim (1975) were employed to develop a checklist. Five different groups participated. Each group was presented the fairy tale separately and drew pictures. A brief description for each group follows.

### Groups

1. Nineteen graduate students, ages twenty-four to forty-two, enrolled in a group counseling course.

2. Four males and four females, ages twelve to fifteen, in grades seven through ten. One male and two females were in divorced families while the other two were from two-parent families.

3. Eight female participants, ages twenty-nine to forty-five, in a support group for displaced homemakers in a funded program to provide them with education and job skills training.

4. Eight members of an overeater group, ages eighteen to twenty-seven, four males and four females. All had completed high school, five had one or more years in college, and one had a master's degree.

5. Eight female therapy clients, ages twenty-six to forty-five, exhibiting behavioral symptoms of eating disorders. Seven were white and one was black.

### Procedure

Participants were asked to close their eyes and listen to the reading of the fairy tale. Afterward they were requested to draw two scenes they felt important in the fairy tale.

### Results

Tables 11-1 and 11-2 present a breakdown of symbols into existential or developmental issues by group. The division into issues is not altogether clear for some items, for example, "struggle for independence," and was an arbitrary decision by the author.

**Table 11.1**
**Comparison of Existential Issues by Groups**

| Existential Issues | Grad. Students | Adolescents | Displaced Home-makers | Overeaters | Eating Disorders |
|---|---|---|---|---|---|
| Death anxiety | 0 | 87 | 37 | 75 | 0 |
| Fear of being deserted | 16 | 62 | 87 | 87 | 28 |
| Achieving higher humanity (acquiring treasures) | 0 | 12 | 25 | 50 | 28 |
| Reducing isolation (returning home safely) | 37 | 25 | 75 | 50 | 28 |
| Successful transition (crossing water) | 5 | 12 | 25 | 0 | 14 |
| The need to find oneself (lost in the forest) | 31 | 50 | 62 | 62 | 28 |
| Failure to meet safety needs (crumbs on path) | 10 | 25 | 12 | 12 | 0 |
| Superior benevolent power (bird on roof, white duck) | 5 | 12 | 25 | 25 | 0 |
| Assuming responsibility (bringing treasure home) | 6 | 12 | 37 | 12 | 18 |

**Table 11.2**
**Comparison of Developmental Issues by Groups**

| Developmental Issues | Grad Students | Adolescents | Displaced Home-makers | Overeaters | Eating Disorders |
|---|---|---|---|---|---|
| Separation anxiety | 37 | 75 | 75 | 100 | 0 |
| Anxiety about being devoured | 5 | 25 | 37 | 25 | 0 |
| Fear of not being fed (oral greediness) | 5 | 50 | 12 | 87 | 43 |
| Struggle for independence | 47 | 62 | 87 | 62 | 14 |
| Destructive oral desires (eating gingerbread house) | 0 | 37 | 0 | 37 | 14 |
| Ineffectual father | 21 | 25 | 37 | 25 | 28 |
| Controlling evil/destructivc aspccts of personality (killing witch) | 10 | 62 | 25 | 37 | 14 |
| Attractiveness of giving in to oral greediness (gingerbread house) | 5 | 37 | 25 | 50 | 28 |
| Goal directed behavior versus instinctual impulses or wish-fulfilling fantasies (tricking witch into oven, substitution of bone for finger) | 16 | 62 | 25 | 37 | 0 |
| Individuation (separate crossing of water on duck) | 0 | 12 | 25 | 12 | 14 |

Table 11-3 presents a partial list of scenes drawn by participants. Of the adolescents 62 percent drew "Pushing the witch into the oven"; 37 percent of displaced homemakers drew "Returning home"; 37 percent of overeaters drew "The Gingerbread House"; 26 percent of graduate students drew "Returning Home"; and 42 percent of the eating disorder group drew "The Gingerbread House". While these percentages represent the largest proportions for each group, of more interest may be the ones that were drawn by the fewest as the issues contained in these may be unexpected. For example, the adolescent who drew

"Asking the Duck for a Ride" would be further along in development, and the member of overeaters who drew "Pushing the Witch into the Oven" may have better control of destructive desires or tendencies, and so on. (See Table 11.3) Group members may not have become fully aware of completing a developmental task, and the fairy tale drawing can contribute to making that awareness more conscious.

## FINDINGS FROM THE LITERATURE

Fairy tales present messages on different levels and the metaphors are left open to interpretation by the individual. Even the same story will produce different meanings for the same individual at different points in his or her life. Interpretations of symbols and metaphors can be suggested; however, the individual tends to impose his or her own unique interpretation according to current experiencing and/or past events, especially unresolved issues. Fairy tales allow each person to find his or her own unique solution by reflecting what the story implies about him or her, and his or her inner conflicts, at this moment in their life. The actual content may have nothing to do with external life but may be a metaphor for inner life. The tale may point the way to solving or understanding incomprehensible and heretofore unsolvable problems. Thiessen (1988) points this out in his discussion, "The importance of metaphors in fairy tales in promoting ego strength, values and well-being.

Although Lubetsky (1989) focused his article on children, the same premises could apply to adolescents and adults. He noted that children usually do not respond to direct queries about their feelings. Fairy tales could be used to allow the child to reduce anxiety, fulfill fantasies, reflect on earlier times, and/or confront real conflicts in development. Adolescents and adults respond much as children do to fairy tales (Brown, 1993).

Brandt (1983) carried the idea a little further when she proposed that fairy tales mirror developmental struggles of childhood and suggest models for resolving these conflicts. Her work focused on separation-individuation issues for borderline adolescents, and use of fairy tales as reflective of both the issues and resolution.

Lehmkuhl (1988) describes fairy tales used in psychotherapy as aids to clarification of inner and socially based human problems. He suggests that fairy tales can also assist in integrating all aspects of personality, "including the unconscious."

Bettelheim (1975) felt that fairy tales allowed for reexperiencing early object-relations in a safe environment, supported the importance of externalization of conflicts with self, allowed for internalization of polarities such as the "good and bad mother," showed how personality integration could be accomplished (e.g., cooperation between conflicted parts of self), and modeled how to achieve autonomy.

**Table 11-3**
**Scenes Drawn by Participants**

| | |
|---|---|
| Gingerbread House | Pushing the witch into the oven (appeared in all groups) |
| Hansel and Gretel in the forest with a fire | Hansel and Gretel returning home |
| Dropping bread crumbs on the path | Dropping pebbles on the path |
| One child on the duck crossing water, the other on the shore | Bringing jewels home |
| Parents leaving Hansel and Gretel in forest | The bird in the forest |

Metaphors and symbols in fairy tales are not limited in meaning. There are multiple meanings which allow the individual to gain a better understanding of self by choosing the one that is most useful to him or her. For example, stepmothers are found in many fairy tales and can be interpreted in numerous ways. Radomisli (1981) interpreted the stepmother as the vehicle to protect both the mother and the child from the child's anger by projecting it onto the "stepmother," or bonding mother and child by showing the negative side of any mother substitute. Thiessen (1988) saw the stepmother as a way of showing a mother who did not want to be a mother. Cashdan (1988) proposed that the stepmother symbol provides the split between the "good" and "bad" mother which allows the integration of both, while Bettelheim (1975) felt that the image helped the child preserve the "good" mother without contamination from the "bad" mother.

## PROCESS OF A FAIRY TALE

Fairy tales usually begin when the central figure(s) is made aware that he/she needs to do something. The character "sets forth," is lured or seduced, is carried away, or in some way voluntarily proceeds to the "threshold or gate" to action. There is usually a guardian of the passage who seeks to prevent entrance, and the central figure and guardian engage in a literal or figurative battle. If the protagonist wins, he/she proceeds to an unfamiliar situation, where he/she faces tests of suitability and magical aids or helpers appear. If the tests or tasks are successfully completed there are rewards, recognition, and/or gifts. As the character returns to the threshold to go back to the place from whence he/she came, he/she has been transformed by the experiences. Thus, one learns that problems are faced by everyone and are capable of being satisfactorily resolved.

### Messages in Fairy Tales

Messages in fairy tales seem to have meanings for people throughout their life. These messages are especially relevant when the familiar has been outgrown; old concepts, ideals, and patterns of relating no longer are satisfactory; and/or the individual is on the threshold of change. Issues such as separation, individuation, sexual awakening, assuming of responsibility, awareness of personal death or nonbeing, can arise at any time throughout one's life and are capable of being expressed in a fairy tale.

There are also common symbols that act as metaphors throughout life. They have relevance for children as well as for adolescents and adults, although they may apply to very different circumstances or situations. Some examples follow:

Forest or wood--an individual's life.

Path--the future.

Lost in forest or wood--one's search for meaning, understanding, seeking to find one's self or way.

Beasts (e.g., wolf, fox)--dissociated, unacknowledged, unacceptable parts of self. When beasts have a "disgusting appearance," they represent the "unconscious deep" wherein are hoarded all of the rejected, unadmitted, unrecognized, unknown, or undeveloped factors, laws, and elements of existence (Campbell, 1973).

Sleeping princes or princesses--unrealized possibilities or potentials.

Witch--destructive aspects of self.

Stepmother--the "not good enough mother."

Helpers, such as birds--benevolent powers that watch over and protect.

Wandering--latency or a waiting period: one is not yet ready to ascend to the next level.

Jewels/rewards--recognition of accomplishment.

Leaving home--becoming independent; separation and individuation.

Swallowed by wolf or other animal--annihilation until readiness to be transformed to a higher plane, or to the next level.

Body of water, such as a pond--emotional life.

Wells--unconscious, container of id impulses and source of creativity.

Red--passion, onset of menses, sexual desire.

Dwarfs--remaining in a child state.

## USING FAIRY TALES IN GROUP COUNSELING

### Purpose(s)

The decision to use a fairy tale in group is made after careful consideration of the purpose for using one, and the psychological readiness of group members. The leader should have a clear purpose that can be communicated to members, such as "The group seems to be going around in circles over this issue and I would like to try an indirect expressive technique to see whether we can break out of this circular discussion." Because fairy tales address basic developmental and existential issues, the leader should have a very good sense of members' ability to handle emergence of these issues at this stage of their counseling.

### Issues or Conditions

Some common conditions that suggest using fairy tales are members' unawareness of basic issues and their impact on current functioning; highlighting of commonalities; suggestions of ways of overcoming impasses; and interruption of storytelling. Often the group leader is aware of basic unresolved developmental issues of group members that continue to have a significant impact on functioning and relationships. For example, it may be obvious that several group members have not successfully completed separation and individuation. They may even be able to accept that they have not done so on an intellectual level but have not integrated the idea on the emotional level so that they can begin to complete the process. Choosing a fairy tale that has a theme of successful completion of separation and individuation could help begin the process.

Because members come to the group with differing concerns and from different situations, they may not be able to recognize and accept the commonalities that exist between them. The manifestations of the developmental and/or existential issues may be significantly different, and this obscures the universality. When the leader recognizes that there are these basic commonalities and that group members are failing to recognize and accept them, a fairy tale can be introduced to highlight these commonalities.

Quite often groups encounter an impasse as the discussion appears to become circular. While there is certainly emotional blocking and resistance, the situation is frustrating to both the leader and members. Many times simply pointing out what is happening is not sufficient to overcome the impasse. Members have to be shown how to get around the blocks and resistances in a way that is nonthreatening and safe. A fairy tale allows very basic and sensitive material to be encountered in a way that is nonthreatening. By expressing difficult emotions around basic developmental and/or existential issues through a fairy tale, members can better deal with their personal emotions and issues.

When a group leader becomes aware that members are storytelling and wish to block or interrupt, a fairy tale can be introduced as a way to focus on basic issues that the member(s) is (are) trying to convey. This is most useful when several members have essentially the same issue, but very different situations or circumstances, and begin to storytell in order to ensure that their uniqueness is understood by all. The fairy tale not only interrupts the storytelling, it also highlights commonalities.

### Group Theme

It is also important to select a fairy tale that meets the purpose as well as having a theme that is relevant for group members. There are times when the group leader has not had sufficient time to allow all basic issues for members to emerge and must proceed on the basis of insufficient knowledge. Even when it may appear that there are some members who do not have the issue or theme personally, the leader will usually find that these members will still be able to gain something from the fairy tale.

### Tales, Themes and Symbols

Table 11.4 on pages 140 through 143 lists fairy tales, underlying themes or messages, and major symbols or metaphors that are intended to serve as suggestions. These were developed building on the common metaphors of Campbell (1973), Bettelheim (1975), and Jung (1958).The group leader is encouraged to read the fairy tales for him or herself to determine their suitability, and to discern additional themes, messages, and uses for specific conditions.

## GUIDELINES FOR USING FAIRY TALES

### Gather Materials

After selecting a fairy tale, gather materials needed for members to draw. (See Chapter 7 for suggested list) Before introducing the tale, tell members what you propose to do and ask whether they wish to participate in the activity. Generally, you will be reading the tale while they listen with their eyes closed, and when you are through, they will be asked to draw scenes from the tale. The overall goal or objective need not be discussed at this time unless it will add to the experience.

### Distribute Materials

Pass out materials before beginning to read. Each group member should receive two sheets of paper and either have a set of colors, such as felt tip markers, or share a set with another person. It is helpful if there are desks or some sort of flat surface on which to draw. The paper can be taped to the walls for drawing if oil pastels, chalk pastels, or crayons are used. Felt tip markers usually have to be held with the tip pointing down to be effective, hence they usually aren't appropriate for drawing on paper on the walls.

### Read Fairy Tale

Read the fairy tale slowly as if you were reading to a group of rapt listeners. Change the tone and tempo when appropriate, and even try to sound different for the various characters when they are talking. Let feeling creep into your voice, for example, when an exciting event occurs sound excited. Most of the fairy tales are short and will take five to fifteen minutes to read.

When the tale is done, ask members to open their eyes and to draw two scenes from the tale. Any two scenes will be acceptable. After the drawings are complete, ask members to give each a title. Time should be allowed for each member to share at least one of the drawings with the group.

### Processing the Experience

There are two parts to processing the drawings: identification of symbols and their personal associations, and associations with current experiencing or functioning. It is extremely important that members be given an opportunity to explain their pictures in the group and to clarify the meaning of the titles given the picture. Often the title is more revealing of underlying issues and current problems than the picture.

The leader may wish to construct a short list of major symbols embedded in the fairy tale that is used. This list can be used in clarifying and expanding on elements in the picture. While the pictures are not being analyzed as they would be by an art therapist, they are being analyzed by the group member who drew them. Focusing on certain symbols and suggested meanings and associations helps members to understand better what some ongoing issues may be as well as pinpointing current concerns that they were only dimly aware of, or of which they were aware.

As members tell about their pictures the leader should ask clarifying questions and seek to expand and deepen the experience. Pay close attention to the impact of the questioning and be alert to those areas that are sensitive and/or threatening to the member. Other members can join in the exploration by reporting the impact of the picture on them but not in interpreting the symbols. This is also an opportunity for similarities to be highlighted. A wealth of material rich in potential can be revealed.

**Table 11-4**
**Tales, Themes and Suggested Meanings**

| Themes | Title | Major Symbols/Metaphors |
|---|---|---|
| | **"The Three Little Pigs"** | |
| Controlling id impulses<br>Getting in touch with reality<br>Learning responsibility<br>Choosing duty over pleasure | | *Lean-to-shack of straw*--id impulses<br>*Brick house*--superego influenced aspect of self<br>*Wolf*--asocial, unconscious destructive aspects of self<br>*Playing*--choosing pleasure over responsibility<br>*Turnips, apples, trip to fair*--appeal to desire for pleasure over responsibility |
| | **"Queen Bee"** | |
| Separation<br>Individuation<br>Controlling impulses<br>Getting in touch with inner resources<br>Unifying conflicting parts of self | | *Helpful animals*--inner aspects that help to master developmental issues<br>*Brothers*--immature parts of self<br>*Turned to stone*--inability to respond to higher values |
| | **"Jack and the Beanstalk"** | |
| Becoming an adult<br>Resolving issues with father<br>Nurturing oneself | | *Cow ceasing to give milk*--weaning<br>*Talking musical instrument*--beauty, art, higher things in life, gaining full humanity<br>*Ogre*--seeing oneself in father<br>*Beans*--the way to achieve the next level<br>*Hen*--all physical needs can now be satisfied |

| Theme | Title | Major Symbols/Metaphors |
|---|---|---|
| | **"Snow White"** | |
| Sexual awakening<br>Latency<br>Reaching for a higher stage of maturity | | *White snow*--innocence<br>*Red blood*--sexual desire<br>*Dwarfs*--childhood before puberty<br>*Apple*--love and sex<br>*Stepmother*--aspects of inner conflict<br>*Eating the apple*--death of childhood<br>*Raven*--mature consciousness<br>*Hunter*--protector, control of asocial and violent tendencies<br>*Reawakening*--reaching a higher stage of maturity |
| | **"Cinderella"** | |
| Readiness to move to another level of development<br>Sibling rivalry<br>Belief in oneself | | *White bird*--hope, belief in self, one's spirit<br>*Slipper*--femininity<br>*Tree planted on grave*--the memory of the idealized mother<br>*Fairy godmother*--benevolent spirit<br>*Stepsisters*--disowned parts of self<br>*Mice, pumpkin*--helpful inner resources |
| | **"Sleeping Beauty"** | |
| Latency<br>Conflicted parts of self<br>The need to protect | | *Fairies*--split parts of self<br>*Hundred years' sleep*--time of quiet growth and preparation for the next stage<br>*Hidden chamber*--formerly inaccessible parts of self<br>*Wall of thorns*--becoming sexually aware before one is physically and emotionally ready |
| | **"Jorinda and Joringel"** | |
| Sexual awakening<br>Controlling desires | | *Witch*--destructive desires<br>*Maidens into birds*--protecting until ready for next level<br>*Turtle doves*--guides |

**Table 11.4 continued**

| Themes | Title | Major Symbols/Metaphors |
|---|---|---|
| | **"Jorinda and Joringel" (continued)** | |
| Protecting child from adult actions | | *Strange village*--becoming aware of others<br>*Spending time as a shepherd*--learning to assume<br>*Blood red flower containing a pearl*--sexual awareness |
| | **"The Three Spinning Fairies"** | |
| The price paid for talent | | *Three fairies*--parts of self that are split off and unrecognized |
| Using all parts of self | | *Lazy girl*--unaccepted part of self |
| | **"The Three Children of Fortune"** | |
| Achieving autonomy | | *Cock, scythe, cat*--conflicted parts of self |
| Separation and individuation | | *Wandering*--learning to find one's way |
| Creative responses | | |
| | **"Red Riding Hood"** | |
| Learning to recognize | | *Red*--intense emotion, becoming an adult |
| Reality | | *Gathering flowers*--ambivalence about pleasure versus responsibility |
| Delay of pleasure | | *Hunter*--protector, rescuer<br>*Cut out of wolf's stomach*--rebirth |
| Recognizing danger | | *Wolf*--animalistic tendencies that seduce one from living constructively |
| Struggle between the desire to do the right thing and the unconscious wish to win over others | | |
| | **"Hansel and Gretel"** | |
| Separation | | *Gingerbread house*--destructive oral desires |
| Individuation | | *Witch*--destructive parts of self<br>*Killing the witch*--controlling destructive parts of self |

| Theme | Title | Major Symbols/Metaphors |
|---|---|---|
| | **"Hansel and Gretel" (continued)** | |
| Controlling self-destructive desires or tendencies<br><br>Interdependence | | *Bread crumbs on path*--failure to meet safety needs<br>*Stones on path*--meeting safety needs<br>*Lost in forest*--need to find oneself<br>*Hansel in cage*--struggle for independence<br>*Bird on roof and in the forest, duck*--benevolent protectors<br>*Crossing water separately on the duck*--achieving individuation<br>*Bringing treasure home*--assuming responsibility<br>*Acquiring jewels*--the next level of maturity |

# 12

# MOVEMENT

## USING THE BODY IN GROUP

### Definitions

Movement, as an expressive process, involves understanding messages that the body sends, structuring situations that evoke movement reflective of inner processes, and having a capacity to be sensitive to the way the body speaks of personal experiencing. Berger and Leventhal (1992) say:

> The body is the vessel, the most fundamental way that we experience ourselves. In our time of emphasis on verbal, cognitive process, the body and its wisdom have become a personal and cultural shadow, and dance/movement therapy seeks to bring out the light in the body, assisting individuals to be more fully themselves, to make soulful self-contact and to extend this vitality and consciousness into their world.

Kepner (1993) proposes that "clients are often at odds with their existence as physical beings," and that therapists also approach therapy from the same dissociated state. Clients, according to Kepner, as well as others, disown aspects of self by pretending that it does not exist (repression and denial), projecting it on to others, and keeping it out of awareness. This is also true for the body. Clients may separate awareness of body from self in response to distressing events that are experienced physically, such as abuse. It is common for people to speak of a body part as hurting rather than saying something like, "I hurt and it is located in my head." Healing the split between mind and body demands that the disowned aspects of self be brought into awareness so they can be integrated.

Kepner (1993) defines the tasks of the therapist as follows:

1. To work with the body to restore contact with body processes.

2. To develop a verbal vocabulary to describe body experience and clarify the meaning of movements, sensations, and other nonverbal processes.

3. To establish a relationship (dialogue) between the split-off parts of the self.

4. To work through unfinished situations so that the disowned functions are assimilated back into the self, the range of possible responses is expanded, and a new creative adjustment is possible.

Berber (1992) describes Isadora Duncan's perception of movement and the child as being one in which the child gets to know who he/she is through the body; and through a series of sequential movements, he/she expresses connected thought patterns. As movements become more complex, the mind and body become more integrated, and there is greater understanding as well as more expression.

The value of movement as an expressive process is perceived by therapists from many theoretical orientations. For example, Tyler (1980), a gestalt therapist, notes, "Using our bodies in new ways may promote awareness more quickly and energetically than verbal experiences alone." Daniels and Horowitz in (1984) propose that the way one moves and holds the body tells much about how he/she perceives him or herself and feels. Reich (1949) maintained that a healthy person displays graceful, rhythmic flow of movement and that character armor results in rigid, tense movements and body postures.

## THEORETICAL PERSPECTIVES

### Dance/Movement

Four theoretical approaches to dance therapy appear to have application to the use of movement in group counseling: Chase, Jungian, developmental, and gestalt. Each has a different goal, set of techniques, and expectation of the counselor.

### Chase

The Chase approach highlights techniques used by the counselor to deepen his/her understanding of the client's experiencing. The client is worked with in terms of where he/she is at that moment regarding energy level and range of emotions. For example, a depressed client with little affect would begin movements or dance in a more restricted way than an anxious client who expresses more affect. The counselor mirrors movements and interacts with the client while moving in order to empathize better. By doing so, energy levels become higher or more manageable and range of emotion increases. Sensations associated with movement are highlighted and can be more easily incorporated into experiencing. The assumptions are that mirroring movements can promote empathy and that seeing one's movements mirrored allows one to access deeper feelings and increase awareness of them, and this awareness leads to more understanding.

### Jungian

The Jungian approach assumes the counselor has been trained in understanding and using Jungian concepts. Movement is perceived to be an expression of the client's inner experiencing on both the personal unconscious and collective unconscious levels. The counselor interprets the client's movements in Jungian terms.

### Developmental

Developmental theory proposes that one's developmental level is revealed through his or her movements. Siegel (1980) asserts that "development of mobility is connected with physical maturation, of course, but it does carry identifiable, phase-specific patterns." She goes on to point out that phase-specific patterns associated with developmental levels, such as rigid spines and body posture of a toddler observed in obsessive-compulsion identified with the anal phase or developmental level, leads to the hypothesis of "the presence of a somatic crystallization of the fixation point." From this point, it proceeds to propose that "the way a person moves also reveals the time in his (her) life his (her) major conflicts were formed." Movement in group counseling then becomes the mechanism by which the muscular tension caused by the original event or situation around the conflict is released and connected with the past and present. This linking is accomplished by the counselor's assessing the client's developmental level by observing his or her movement, and then relating to him or her at that level through mirroring and carefully designed reciprocal movement.

### Gestalt

The gestalt approach to movement therapy relies on the therapist's extending the client's awareness and expression of his/her conflicts by focusing on integrating body movements into a connected expression of inner and outer experiencing. Tyler (1980) describes her purposes and process of dance-movement in therapy as guiding the client to touch others, to become aware of how he/she perceives him or herself with others, and to establish an integrated experience of inner and outer worlds. Dance and movement are used as sources of pleasure, a stimulus to self-awareness, a way to dissolve barriers and to contact continuing needs. This use of dance and movement relies heavily on gestalt concepts of figure-ground, recapturing of fragmented parts of self, polarities, and unfinished business.

### Movement in Therapy

Movement is used in therapy in a variety of ways but dance is the mode most often described in the literature. Siegel (1980) defines *dance-movement therapy* as "a form of psychotherapy in which the therapist utilizes movement interaction as the primary means for establishing therapeutic goals." She proposes that movement is reflective of personality and that the interpersonal relationship with the therapist is established through movement. Dance-movement therapists consider the mode to be a process by which inner conflicts and experiences can be expressed without overwhelming clients with tensions, anxieties, and affect. Dance-movement therapy is used to disperse bottled-up, overwhelming affect; to build motor skills; and to facilitate building of body image. (Schilder 1950)

Siegel (1980) feels that developmental levels, expression of internal conflict, and the receptor imprinted with reactions to all past and present experiences can be determined with dance-movement. Tyler (1980) uses movement-dance in therapy as a means of experiencing pleasure, stimulating self-awareness, and dissolving barriers. Others use movement-dance to unite feeling and sensation functions (Jung 1958), gain greater control of isolated body parts, improve body image, achieve controlled emotional release, and become more socially adept.

## OTHER USES FOR MOVEMENT

### Mind-Body Connections

Goleman and Gurin (1993) assert that mind/body approaches should become a routine part of medical care for the following reasons: Research has demonstrated that mind/body approaches have potential for reducing pain and improving the quality of life for those with chronic diseases, can help control or reverse some underlying disease processes, reduce the effects of stress, entail little risk of causing physical or psychological damage, and have low costs and easy applications.

*Relaxation.* Benson (1984) has studied the effects of relaxation on various conditions, for example, hypertension, since 1967 and consistently found that relaxing has a positive effect on the functioning of the body: such as lowering the level of lactate in the bloodstream, which is associated with peace and tranquility; producing more low frequency alpha, theta, and delta waves in the brain wave patterns, indicating more rest and relaxation; causing slower, deeper breathing; and decreasing heart rate and muscle tension. Some people have even shown a decrease in blood pressure. Relaxation techniques that have been shown effective include transcendental meditation and prayer, yoga, autogenic training, progressive muscle relaxation, and hypnosis.

*Meditation.* Jon Kabat-Zinn (1993) conducts intensive training in "mindfulness meditation" for patients with a variety of disorders, such as cancer, heart disease, hypertension, and chronic pain. Research on the technique done to date suggests that this process has a positive effect for those suffering from stress-related conditions. Mindful meditation is an outgrowth of a Buddhist practice that involves focusing on your current experiencing instead of blocking out physical discomfort and distracting thoughts. The technique proposes that one embrace tension, anxiety, distress, frustration, and so forth, rather than trying to ignore, suppress, deny, or in some way remove the condition.

*Mindful meditation uses three major practices*: body scan, sitting meditation, and hatha yoga positions. *Body scan* involves becoming aware of each region of your body and the physical sensations experienced for each, at that moment. This is done systematically, beginning with a focus on breathing and becoming aware of your toes, moving on to other parts, and ending with the top of your head. *Sitting meditation* begins with sitting straight, focusing on your breathing, and allowing yourself to experience what is happening with your mind and your body. *Hatha yoga* used in mindful meditation, includes concentrating on the experiencing, such as breathing and physical sensations, while doing the stretching and bending exercises.

## GUIDELINES FOR USING MOVEMENT IN GROUP

### Benefit For All Members

There are a variety of movement and dance expressive processes that hold potential as enhancers of counseling. However, most of them are appropriate for individual counseling and/or work with individuals in a group setting. There are considerably fewer that are appropriate for use with the group-as-a-whole because the focus is on deepening and expanding an experience for one individual at a time. When selecting an exercise or technique always keep in mind that the purpose of the experience is that all members of the group benefit as well as providing some benefit for the group process. Some group-as-a-whole objectives could be to stimulate self-awareness for group members and at the same time dissolve barriers and highlight similarities, express moods, tell a story, contact disowned parts of self, and have fun.

### Gather Materials

After determining the objective(s), the leader should gather any needed materials prior to the session using movement. Materials such as musical selections, tape or compact disc player, masks, and props such as tables are examples for use with movement-dance. It may be helpful to consult a musician when using music to evoke a particular mood as they usually have experience and knowledge of musical works that are appropriate. Further, they can suggest selections where the emphasis will be on the objective and not on the music.

### Explain Process

Explain the exercise and process to group members before beginning any movement-dance experience. Many members will have some resistance to participating and this reluctance should be expressed openly. The leader has a responsibility to present the exercise in a nonthreatening way with a definite purpose and benefit to the group member delineated. Introduce group members to a simple nonthreatening exercise first before beginning other movements. A relaxation or stretching exercise that lasts two to three minutes may be enough to make them feel more comfortable.

### Phases

There are three phases to a movement-dance experience: warm-up, working, and processing. *Warm-up* refers to loosening the body, overcoming self-consciousness, and relaxing. This phase brings members to the present and heightens awareness of bodily sensations. It gives the leader an opportunity to teach members strategies for reducing tension that can be used in other situations: strategies such as breathing exercises, meditation, stretching, and development of awareness of bodily blocks to energy.

The *working phase* uses creative movement to elicit imagery, memories, and fantasies that provide clues to repressed or denied parts of self, unfinished business, and unintegrated polarities. During this phase movements are spontaneous, and can be used to tell a story or to act out an emotion. Exercises such as pulling strings and following the movement fall into this category. The third phase, *processing*, is extremely important as this is the time when group members integrate the inner and outer experiencing, analyze their responses, and examine their associations. This is the phase when meaning and understandings become clearer.

## EXAMPLES FOR USING MOVEMENT IN GROUP

### Pulling Strings

*Objectives*. To increase awareness of how it feels when others control us; to become aware of how it feels to allow ourselves to be controlled; to become aware of how it feels just to "let go."

Group members can pair off or form a circle. They are then instructed to imagine that there are strings attached to their knees, wrists, and head. As they stand there, no one has a grip on the strings and so members allow the muscles of the body to go limp and floppy. If there are partners, one member mimes picking up the strings and pulling them to make the other member (puppet) walk, run, and sit down. After a few minutes, they switch roles. If the members are in a circle, each should walk, run, and sit imagining that someone is holding the strings that control his or her movements. Processing focuses on feelings experienced during each of the activities: being limp and floppy (letting go of tension), being controlled by someone else, and so forth. The discussion can emphasize the extent and degree to which members allow others to "pull their strings" and the impact on their functioning and relationships.

### Relaxation

*Objective*. To experience release of muscle tension.

*Note*. Members should be instructed to do only that which is comfortable for them. If any pain is experienced, they should stop at once.

*Standing stretch 1*: Members are instructed to stand up, raise both arms over their heads, and reach for the roof. As they reach up, have them gently arch their backs and stretch their fingers out as far as they can. This pose should be held for ten seconds, if they can comfortably do so. Some may find it beneficial to do this exercise more than once.

*Standing stretch 2*: Members are instructed to stand up, clasp their hands behind their back below the waist, pull the clasped hands down, and hold for ten seconds. Note postures, and encourage members to stand as straight as possible when doing this stretch for maximum benefits.

*Sitting stretch*: Members are instructed to sit up straight, move shoulders back as far as they can, and hold for six to seven seconds before releasing. Then, instruct members to bring their shoulders forward, hunching them as much as possible; hold for six to seven seconds; and then release them. For the last sitting stretch, instruct members to bring their shoulders up to their ears as high as they can, hold for six to seven seconds, and then release. These can be repeated if more relaxation is desired.

*Face and throat stretch:* Members are instructed to stand up, yawn as widely as possible, and then release. After doing this twice, they are instructed to make a noise when they yawn. This is also done twice.

*Standing breathing exercise*: Members are instructed to stand straight with arm straight down, knees slightly bent, and feet about ten to twelve inches apart. They are also free to find the position that is most comfortable for them. They are instructed to close their eyes and become aware of where they are tense in their body. Give the following instructions in your own words: "As you become aware of the tension in your body, allow your breathing to become deep and even. Concentrate on breathing, deeply and evenly. If you become aware that your breaths are shallow and/or uneven, consciously change them to become deep and even." Give these instructions quietly with sufficient pauses between. Allow enough time for members to experience the activity before instructing them to open their eyes and take their seats.

*Sitting breathing exercise:* Instruct members to sit up as straight as they can, feet flat on floor, with hands on knees. Have them close their eyes and give the same instructions as used for the standing breathing exercise. After members are familiar with this exercise, the leader may wish to add an affirming statement that members can concentrate on while doing the exercise, such as "I allow my body to be still, my thoughts to become quiet, my muscles to relax, my breathing to become deep and even."

### Following and Mirroring

*Objectives*: To become aware of what emotional states one is experiencing at the moment; to experience controlled emotional release; to obtain feedback on how one is perceived by others.

*Sitting Imitation:* The leader describes the exercise to members by saying that one member will begin the exercise by sitting in a chair, assuming a position that portrays how he/she is feeling. The next member mimics the position and then assumes a position that portrays how he/she is feeling. The mirroring and assuming of positions reflective of inner experiencing continue until all members have participated. The leader can begin or end the exercise and is encouraged to participate.

*Follow the Movement*: The leader selects a piece of music that is somewhat neutral in that it is neither too fast nor too slow, not a current popular tune or in some way too energizing or distracting. The focus is on the movement, not the music.

The directions are given before turning on the music and beginning the exercise. Members are told that one member will begin the process by moving to the music. The next member must imitate that movement and then change positions or movement to one that is unique to him or her, and so on, until all members have had a chance to participate. The exercise may be more effective if members are asked to use a movement that illustrates how they are feeling. It is most important to observe the unique movements carefully and to have processing emphasize feelings and emotions experienced while waiting, mirroring the other movement, doing their unique movement, observing others, and afterward. The impact of the music should be explored also.

*Follow the movement 2*: Members are instructed to line up on one side of the room. The directions for the exercise are for each member to move to the other side of the room in turn. The only limitation is that each member must move across the room in a different way than did any other member. Processing should focus on observations, feelings while waiting and while moving across the room, and current feelings. Ask what was most difficult about the exercise.

# REFERENCES


Acuff, F. (1993). *How to Negotiate Anything with Anyone Anywhere Around the World.* Amacon, New York.

Agazarian, Y. (1992). "Contemporary theories of group psychotherapy: A systems approach to the group-as-a-whole." *International Journal of Group Psychotherapy 4.* (2): 177-204.

Ahnsen, A. (1977). *Psycheye.* New York, Brandon House.

Ahnsen, A. (1988). "Prolucid dreaming." *Journal of Mental Imagery 12* 1: 57-70.

Assagioli, R. (1965). *Psychosynthesis: A Manual of Principles and Techniques.* Hobbs, Dorman, New York.

Banet, A. and J. Jones (1976). *1976 Annual for Group Facilitators.* J. Jones and W. Pfeiffer editors. University Associates, LaJolla, California.

Barrineau, P. (1991). Person-centered dream work. *Journal of Humanistic Psychology* 32 1: 90-105.

Baylor, G. and D. Deslauriers (1987). "Dreams as problem solving: A method of study: Part II: The oral defense dream." *Imagination, Cognition and Personality* 7 1: 23-45

Benson, H. (1993). "The relaxation response." *Mind/Body Medicine.* D. Goleman and J. Gwin editors. Consumer Reports Books, Yonkers, New York.

Berber, M. (1992). "Isadora Duncan and the creative source of dance therapy." *American Journal of Dance Therapy* 14 (2): 95-110.

Berber, M. & M. Leventhal (1992). "Editorial." *American Journal of Dance Therapy.* 14 (2): 71-72.

Berman, S. (1982). *Words, Meanings and People.* International Society for General Semantics, San Francisco.

Berne, E. (1973). *Principles of Group Treatment.* Grove Press, New York.

Bettelheim, B. (1975). *The Uses of Enchantment.* New York Vintage Books, New York.

Brandt, L. (1983). "The fairy tale as paradigm of the separation-individuation crises: Implications for treatment of the borderline adolescent." *Adolescent Psychiatry II:* 75-91.

Brown, N. (1993). "Use of fairy tales in therapy." Paper presented at the American Group Psychotherapy Association National Convention, San Diego, February.

Campbell, J. Jr. (1973). *The Hero with a Thousand Faces*. Princeton University Press, Princeton, New Jersey.

Cashdan, S. (1988). *Object Relations Therapy*. W. W. Norton, New York.

Condrau, G. (1991) "Phenomenological dream interpretation." *Psychoanalysis and Psychotherapy* 9 (1): 56-64.

Corey, G. (1991). *Theory and Practice of Group Counseling* 3rd edition. Brooks/Cole. Pacific Grove, California.

Daniels, V. and L. Horowitz (1984). *Being and Caring,* 2nd. ed. Mayfield, Palo Alto, California.

Darwin, C. (1872). *The Expression of the Emotions in Man and Animals*, fifty impression, 1974. The University of Chicago Press, Chicago and London.

Desoille, R. (1966). *The Directed Daydream*. Psychosynthesis Research Foundation, New York.

Ekman, P. (1965). "Differential communication of affect by head and body cues." *Journal of Personality and Social Psychology* 2: 726-735.

Elliott, J. (1976). *An Outline of Guided Imagery Theory*. Explorations Institute, Berkeley, California.

Feder, B. and R. Rondall (1980). *Beyond the Hot Seat*. Brunner/Mayel, New York.

Feifel, H. (1963). *Taboo topics*. Normal Forberow editor. Atherton Press, New York.

Frankel, K. (1963). *Man's Search for Meaning*. Washington Square Press. New York.

Funk and Wagnall (1963) *Standard College Dictionary*, Funk and Wagnall Co., New York.

Goleman, D. and J. Gurin, editors (1993). *Mind/Body Medicine*. Consumer Reports Books, Yonkers, New York.

Jung, C. G. (1956). *Two Essays on Analytical Psychology*. New York, Meridian Books.

Jung, C. G. (1958). *Man and His Symbols* Dell, New York.

Jung, C. G. (1960). *The Structure and Dynamics of the Psyche*. Pantheon Books, New York.

Kabat-Zinn, J. (1993). "Mindful meditation: Health benefits of an ancient buddhist practice." in *Mind/Body Medicine*. D. Goleman and J. Gurin editors. Consumer Reports Books, Yonkers, New York.

Kepner, J. (1993) *Body Process*. Jossey-Bass, San Francisco.

Klein, M. (1932). *The Psychoanalysis of Children*. Delta Books, New York.

Kline, L. W. and D. E. Johannsen (1935). "Comparative role of the face and of the face-body-hands as aids in identifying emotions." *Journal of Abnormal and Social Psychology* 29: 415.

Lehmkuhl, J. (1988). "From Hans in luck: to superman: The importance of fairy tales in psychotherapy with children." *Acta Paedopsychiatrica* 1 (1): 28-37.

Leuner, H. (1969). "Guided affective imagery." *American Journal of Psychotherapy* 23: 4-21.

Lubetsky, M. (1989). "The magic of fairy tales: Psychodynamic and developmental perspectives." *Child Psychiatry and Human Development* 19 (4): 245-255.

Mack, J. (1970). *Nightmares and Human Conflict*. Houghton Mifflin, Boston.

Mader, T. and D. Mader (1990). *Understanding One Another*. Wm. C. Brown, Dubuque, Iowa.

Matos, L. (1985). "The language of dreams: A psychotherapeutic, transpersonal approach." *Psychiatria Fennica Supplementum* 159-165.

May, R. (1981). *Freedom and Destiny*. Norton 5, New York.

McNiff, S. (1992). *Art as Medicine*. Shambhala, Boston and London.

Mehrabian, A. (1971). *Silent Messages*. Wadsworth, Belmont, California.

Morrison, R. A. (1990). "Dream mapping in chemical dependency recovery." *Alcoholism Treatment Quarterly*, 7 (3): 113-120.

Pease, A. (1984). *Signals*. Bantam Books, New York.

Perls, F. (1970). "Four lectures." *Gestalt Therapy Now*. J. Fagan and I. Sheperd, editors. Harper & Row (Colophon), New York.

Polster, E. and M. Polster (1973). *Gestalt Therapy Integrated*. Brunner/Mayel, New York.

Porter, L. and R. Samovar (1991). "Basic principles of intercultural communication." *Intercultural Communication*. Porter, L. and R. Samovar editors. 6th ed. Wadsworth, Belmont, California.

Progoff, I. (1977). *At a Journal Workshop*. Dialogue House Library, New York.

Radomisli, M. (1981) "Stereotypes, stepmothers and splitting." *The American Journal of Psychoanalysis* 41 (2): 121-127.

Reich, W. (1949). *Character Analysis*. Noonday Press, New York.

Robbins, A. (1980). "Introduction to expressive therapy." *Expressive Therapy*. New York, Human Sciences Press.

Rogers, C. (1951). *Client-Centered Therapy*. Houghton Mifflin, Boston.

Rossman, M. (1993). "Imagery: learning to use the mind's eye." *Mind/Body Medicine*. D. Gelman and J. Gurin editors. Consumer Reports Books, Yonkers, New York.

Ruesch, J. and W. Kees (1956). *Nonverbal Communication*. University of California Press, Berkeley, California.

Sarlin, B. (1991). "Dream appreciation group: A model of stress prevention for medical students." *Group* 15 (3): 181-189.

Schilder, P. (1950). *The Image and Appearance of the Human Body*. International Universities Press, New York.

Schultz, W. (1967). *Joy*. Grove Press, New York.

Shuttleworth-Jordan, A., G. Saayman and P. Faber (1988). "A systematic method for dream analysis in a group setting." *International Journal of Group Psychotherapy* 38 (4): 473-486.

Sourkes, B. (1991). "Truth to life: Art therapy with pediatric oncology patients and their siblings." *Journal of Psychosocial Oncology* 9 (2): 81-96.

St. Clair, M. (1986). *Object Relations and Self Psychology*. Brooks/Cole, Monterey, California.

Thiessen, I. (1988). "The importance of metaphors in fairy tales in promoting ego-strength values and well being." Presented at the annual meeting of the International Council of Psychologists, Singapore.

Tompkins, S. (1963). *Affect-imagery-consciousness*, Vol. II. Springer, New York.

Tyler, D. (1980). "Gestalt movement therapy in groups." *Beyond the Hot Seat*. B. Feder and R. Ronall editors. Brunner/Mayel, New York.

Walrond-Skinner, S. (1986) *Dictionary of Pychotherapy*, Routledge and Kegan Paul, London and New York.

*Webster's New Twentieth Century Dictionary* 2nd. ed. (1983). Simon and Schuster, Cleveland, Ohio.

Winnicott, D. (1989). *Therapeutic Consultations in Child Psychiatry*. Basic Books, New York.

Yalom, I. (1985). *The Theory and Practice of Group Psychotherapy*. Basic Books, New York.

# INDEX

## About the Author

NINA W. BROWN is Professor of Counseling, Darden College of Education, Old Dominion University. She has written extensively on counseling issues, including *Teaching Group Dynamics* (Praeger, 1992) and *Group Counseling for Elementary and Middle School Children* (Praeger, 1994).

ISBN 0-275-95509-5

EAN

9 780275 955090 90000>

HARDCOVER BAR CODE